Table of Contents

ENDLESS SUMMER:
My Life with The Beach Boys

WARNING:

Strong Language/

Content

BY JACK LLOYD

Published in the USA by:

BEARMANOR MEDIA
P.O. BOX 71426
ALBANY, GEORGIA 31708
www.BearManorMedia.com

ISBN-10: 1-59393-113-1 (alk. paper)
ISBN-13: 973-1-59393-113-1 (alk. paper)

Printed in the United States of America.

COPY EDITOR: DAVID W. MENEFEE

BOOK DESIGN AND LAYOUT BY VALERIE THOMPSON

Acknowledgments

I suppose one is generally required to dedicate a book to someone, and there are a few people to whom I owe whatever success and fun I've had over the years.

First is my wife, Phyllis. She has managed to put up with me all these years; she stood by me when I changed occupations, sometimes on a whim, and survived with me during those times when we scuffled financially—mostly because money was not always a motivating factor with me. Phyllis is also the one person who pulled me through when the going got tough.

My kids, Robert and Alison, put up with me not always being there for them, especially when I was on the road. Mostly, what they got out of it were autographed pictures of the rock and roll groups that either opened for The Beach Boys or those Irving Granz and Michael Zugsmith and I produced. I owe a huge debt of thanks to Robert, without whose computer smarts I would have never been able to complete this book.

I also owe Michael Zugsmith a vote of thanks when he stepped up to give me work after a serious auto accident cut down my physical ability to work as an insurance inspector.

Last, but by no means least, I owe a debt of gratitude to David Menefee, the talented author who edited this book. His intelligence and understanding put this effort into a semblance of proper form. He corrected more than a few misused commas, semi-colons, capitalization, and every other English and literary form that I missed in English classes. Thank goodness there are people like David who paid attention and who lived to help all those of us who got by making up the rules as we went.

There must be others to whom I owe thanks; but that would be traveling far afield and probably don't belong in a book about show business. They know who they are because I would hope I've let you know along the way. I owe many, many thanks to all those people who have kept me amused all these years.

Prologue

My personal feeling is that no one ever reads a Prologue, so I had no intention of writing one. Then, I thought I might like to write an Epilogue, but one can hardly write an Epilogue without a Prologue. In any case, it won't be long because I hate long introductions to anything. Okay, okay, sexual foreplay is the one exception. Someone was sure to bring it up.

This book is a sort of journal, with only a passing thought or two as to chronology, but then what's the difference if some things are out of order? Who really cares? Certainly, not I.

The book is about Sex, Drugs, and Rock and Roll. I don't know if it really has much to do with any of those, but I'm told that books sell best if they're about Sex, Drugs, and Rock and Roll. There is almost nothing about drugs, except some pot and a very little cocaine, but mostly wine and liquor. Rock and Roll—there's a lot of that because it takes up a good part of the book.

Sex? Let me say this about sex. It's everywhere you turn in the entertainment business. In the music business, groups like The Beach Boys attracted females from fourteen to forty. It wasn't so much a matter of how, but how many. It was always there. It was almost always there for me if I wanted it even though I was only the producer. However, I found no particular value in delving very deeply into anyone's sexual proclivities, although in a couple of instances I couldn't resist. One must consider the laws of slander. Yes, there are some references to sex, it would be difficult to avoid entirely but I tried not to be overly specific.

Besides, anything I would have written about sex or sexual escapades would also implicate me, even though any reference may not have actually included me, so I tried to be reasonably circumspect. I felt no compunction to write a "kiss and tell" book, because I don't believe it is anyone's business and in the long run, revelations of any sort may hurt someone, so why talk about them, except in the abstract or where it can have no serious ramifications. Considering I had no intent to write about sex, I sure seem to have spent a lot of time not talking about it. So, if it's not a "tell all" book, it turns out to be a "tell some" book. I also use a few nasty words, but mostly in the sense of actual quotations. I hope we're all adults here.

I have left out a lot of stories which may have had some interest to the reader. They were interesting to me and fun when they happened, but once again, the incidents may, in retrospect, have made the protagonists look foolish, or worse. So, why bother? I didn't.

I think there's enough personal business in here to have some fun with. I had fun putting it on paper, and you just might enjoy it, too.

Introduction

As of 2010, there were only two Beach Boys left who could have written an Introduction to this book: Mike Love or Bruce Johnston. The first problem I had was that I no longer had any idea how to contact either of them. After Dennis Wilson did himself in, I spoke briefly with Bruce, but of the others with whom I worked, I would only consider Dick Duryea their Personal Manager. However, Dick became a "behind-the-scenes player," and as highly as I regard him, asking him to write something would hardly be fair. Most of the other people with whom I worked have either passed on were never important enough in my life to ask them to think of something nice to say about me or my writing. Take my word for it. I would just like to thank you for reading, and hope you find something interesting in it.

JACK LLOYD

CHAPTER ONE:
How I Ended Up in Show Business

Going back to my days in junior high school during the nine months I lived in San Francisco, I actually thought I might end up doing something with the "Arts." I wrote one-act plays, which I directed in an English class, mostly to keep from doing the work we were supposed to be doing. My problem was that coming from Chicago, everything we were studying in that class I had already studied the semester before we moved west, so I was bored.

When I finally moved back to Chicago, I put those thoughts aside until my last year in elementary school, when our class decided to produce a pageant of Rogers Park, the neighborhood in which we lived. We—the entire class—made and painted scenery, wrote the play, while most of us acted in it, which awakened the bug. I not only had the job of stage manager, but acted in eight of the sixteen scenes. My life-long friend, Herb Golden (who did go on to become an actor, director, and Emmy Award-winning producer) and I climbed a twenty-four-foot ladder to hang a new curtain in the auditorium and put new gels in the overhead lights.

Somehow or other, it came to me that a great way to meet girls— I was very shy about girls—would to become an actor. I heard that men and women dressed in the same dressing rooms in the theater, and if I became an actor, I was certain to get to see women in less clothing and possibly none at all, and I might actually get to learn about sex. However, it didn't take me very long to figure out that like most everything else I did back then, I could never be dedicated to becoming an actor. Even at that tender age, it was obvious to me that acting took all my concentration and efforts and that just wasn't me. My acting "career" and all else involved with show business got put on hold until my freshman year at the University of Southern California, when I found myself enrolled in a Radio Directing class, working with senior radio acting students. From there, I ended up with three radio shows on the AM station and some acting on the school's FM station. However, thoughts of ending up a radio actor/director left my mind when I decided I couldn't afford to get married if I went to work in radio for $25 a week. Then, fate intervened.

When I was still attending the University of Southern California, I and several friends made a few extra dollars selling souvenir program books at jazz concerts at the Shrine Auditorium. Norman Granz, the man who took jazz out of the joints and on to the concert stage, was a friend of a friend, and he hired a bunch of his young friends and their friends, which somehow got to include me whenever he had a show in Los Angeles. Not really hard work, except on the vocal cords, and it was an easy $15 or $20, big time money for someone living on the $20 a week the government gave veterans for a year. Selling programs was my introduction to the concert world.

Norman Granz had a younger brother, Irving, who eventually went into the concert business. His baptism of fire, so to speak, was the purchase of a date from brother Norman for his client, Ella Fitzgerald. The fact that Norman wouldn't give him a break on Ella's asking price put Irving immediately in the ranks of the professionals. Over the next few years, Irving branched out, particularly with and for The Beach Boys. He would produce fill-in dates for them, using their money. Irving took 10 percent of the gross, an excellent deal for him, although not necessarily for The Beach Boys.

I MEET THE BEACH BOYS

Sometime in the early 1960s, Irving had booked a Beach Boy concert in Long Beach, California, but for whatever reason, he could not make the date himself. He called me and asked if I would supervise the show for him. I agreed, went to Long Beach, introduced myself to the group and to a young Englishman, Ian

Whitcomb, who was the opening act. I took care of the box office, started the show on time, and got the hell out of the way.

It was September 1965, to be exact, and I was suddenly out of work, with nothing to do for the next four months except study for my detective's license, the business I was suddenly out of for reasons which have nothing to do with this book. There I was, sitting around the house, when Irving Granz called.

He said, "Mo (being Mo Ostin, not yet the best record executive who ever lived) tells me you're not working."

"Right," I replied.

"So," he continued, "anything I offer you is more than you're making now."

"Right," I said, unable to deny his logic.

"So, why not come to work for me?"

As I couldn't think of a good reason, I responded, "Okay, Irving, but only until January when I open my own agency."

That is why in September 1965 I found myself in the concert business working for the magnificent sum of $150 a week. Mostly, I did all the office work, wrote all the publicity, kept the books, paid the bills, and sold souvenir books when we had a concert in Los Angeles or nearby. Eventually, I went on tours with or for Irving—selling books or producing, but I am getting ahead.

Irving produced concerts all over the country—we could do that back then—with whichever rock and roll group was currently "hot." He also had, as I have mentioned, a deal with The Beach Boys to produce some of their concerts, finding locations to fill the open dates that their agency had been unable to sell. Economically, it probably made sense for The Beach Boys regardless of their net because they picked up some money when it would have been all outlay having to sit around waiting for their next date.

In the mid to late 1960s, The Beach Boys were *not* at their peak of popularity. It was the time of "message" groups like Country Joe (McDonald) and the Fish, The Jefferson Airplane, Sgt. Barry Sadler and his "Ballad of the Green Beret." The Beach Boys were into fun; not the Haight-Ashbury drug, "drop out, tune in, turn on" scene.

Among the groups Irving bought and produced with his own money were Peter, Paul and Mary, the Righteous Brothers, the

Smothers Brothers, and the Kingston Trio, playing them in places like San Diego, Long Beach, Santa Barbara, and in the case of the Smothers Brothers, Pasadena, home of the Rose Bowl and lots of "old money." We went to those places together, and if we had the souvenir book, I sold them.

Irving had book deals with the Righteous Brothers, Andy Williams, Henry Mancini, The Beach Boys, and Donovan of "Mellow Yellow" fame. Irving also had a deal with promoters Lou Robin and Alan Tinkley to work some of their dates on a fee or a percentage basis. That's how we ended up producing nine Bill Cosby concerts.

I OUTSLICKER A MAJOR UNIVERSITY

One of the Cosby dates was going to be at Ohio State University in Columbus—a sure sell out. I was busy setting up the details that Irving didn't want to handle, writing publicity releases, and placing calls for Irving to radio stations and newspapers when the university contacted us.

The student committee decided they wanted to buy the date. Lou and Alan didn't care and left the decision up to Irving. He saw a way to make money without doing the work and agreed to let them have it, building in a profit for us, Lou, and Alan.

The school, quite naturally, asked for a contract. At that time, we were dealing with one of the better known legal firms in Beverly Hills, so I placed a call and explained the situation to them. By the time we finished the conversation, I said, "Look, forget it, I'll write the contract myself."

When the legal department at OSU got the document, they called me immediately. "Who wrote this?" they asked.

"I did," I responded.

"Do you really expect us to sign it? We've never read a contract this tough."

"Yes," I answered, "if you want Cosby, I do expect you to sign it." They did.

In the summer of 1966, we undertook a major event at the Hollywood Bowl, repeating it at San Francisco's Cow Palace a week later. Irving had produced a similar event at the Bowl in 1965, and while I wasn't officially employed by him yet, I did considerable work on the show. It was called *The Beach Boys Summer Spectacular*, and he used most of the top acts in the country. In 1966, Irving hired hot new acts like Sonny and Cher, Sam the Sham, Dino, Desi, and Billy, and a new kid named Neil Diamond, to whom we paid the munificent sum of $100, which wasn't bad for a kid who just sat on a stool and crooned a few songs.

The 1966 concert also featured The Byrds, Chad and Jeremy, Sir Douglas, Captain Beefheart, and The Lovin' Spoonful, which was the top act in the country that year, and of course, The Beach Boys.

In the fall of 1965, a month or two after I joined him, Irving was scheduled to go on tour with The Beach Boys and me.

CHAPTER TWO:
How to Make a Buck on Someone Else's Dime

Irving's normal routine was to make one swing through the cities we booked, usually five or six dates at a time, to do promotions with newspapers and radio stations, then a week or so before the actual start date of the tour, he'd go cover "our" cities again, ending up at *their* first date. Then, he'd travel with them to every date from then on, all at The Beach Boy's expense. It was a good arrangement for Irving because he lived high on the hog and charged all his expenses to The Beach Boys. It took them a couple more years to realize they weren't getting the best of the deal.

After making a few trips with Irving to sell souvenir books, I got to know the auditorium managers, their salespeople, and local independent booksellers (when the "house" didn't have their own people). It didn't take very much gray matter to figure out that with proper use of those sellers, it would be possible for Irving Granz Productions to net more money if I stayed home and dealt with vendors by telephone. I also got friendly with a man named Lou Gilbert, who handled book sales for Johnny Mathis. Lou got his start as a salesman on the streets of New York selling what he called "Larrys," fake watches to suckers. His training on the streets made him the best book seller in the business. He taught me tricks I could use and how to spot crooks from among the people we used as sellers. Lou did so well that he bought homes in Florida for his kids and dressed in only the finest haberdashery.

There *were* some real advantages to my traveling. First and foremost, Irving could trust me not to screw him on the sales count. Sellers frequently reported receiving fewer books than we sent or would report returns of more books than they actually shipped back. They'd just sell the books and keep the extra money. Then, too, if I was there, I knew precisely how many books were left over and, if I was traveling with The Beach Boys, could ship them ahead on their equipment truck to the next date, or back to Los Angeles. Also, it got me out of the office and I didn't want to give up that perk.

ME IN FOR IRVING / I BEGIN TO LEARN

My first trip with The Beach Boys came when Irving got an emergency call to come home for some personal reason. I flew out on the "red-eye" that same night to meet the group in Kansas City, Missouri. I was to produce that show and then fly on to Philadelphia the next morning to work a Duke Ellington, Ella Fitzgerald concert Irving was handling for his brother, Norman (there was a lull in their constant bickering, I suppose), while Irving flew back to pick up The Beach Boys tour.

Irving instructed me to keep an eye on the ticket manager in Philadelphia because Norman, who managed Ella, thought that somehow he was being cheated. Not that the ticket count didn't match the dollars in the till, but to Norman's trained eye, the last time Ella played Philadelphia, there appeared to be more people in the audience than ticket sales could account for.

The Beach Boys' date went smoothly, and I guess I handled it to everyone's satisfaction. Besides, The Beach Boys had a Road Manager, Dick Duryea, a son of the well-known actor, Dan Duryea, who knew what to do; he certainly knew more than I did at that time, and everything was pretty much under control when I arrived. Practically all I had to do, really, was start the show on time, balance the box office, and pick up the money when it was done.

I returned to the hotel late after the Kansas City concert because I had not yet learned to balance a box office quickly. I was walking to my room to pack for an early morning flight to Philadelphia, when I passed an open door, and of course, looked in. Dennis Wilson, the sex symbol and drummer, saw me and called for me to come join him, which, of course, I did.

Sitting in a chair in the corner was a pleasant looking, grey-haired lady, who turned out to be Audree Wilson, the mother of Dennis, Carl, and Brian. I turned towards Dennis as he jumped into bed and under the covers and was surprised to see a young girl in an advanced state of undress already there.

This seemed somewhat inappropriate to me—that Dennis had this girl all over him while his mother and I, who hardly knew him, watched. I presumed he picked her up at the concert because she certainly hadn't been with the group when I arrived in Kansas City that morning. It wasn't until sometime later that night that Dennis introduced me to Carol—his current wife, who had flown out that afternoon with Audree.

Dennis had already ordered fried chicken and asked me to stick around, talk, and help them eat. I was to learn that Dennis always ordered more than he could possibly eat and always asked people to join him. I begged off for the moment, saying that I had to pack, but promised to return as soon as I finished. I wound up staying with Dennis, his mother, and wife until there was just enough time left for me to shower and change for the flight. Dennis and I became good friends that night. In fact, he became more like a kid brother to me.

I arrived in Philadelphia, very tired, checked into the Belden Stratford hotel that was about a block from the auditorium, and turned on the television. I figured watching a football game would keep me awake until it was time to go to the theater for the first of the two shows that night.

Besides, I wanted to be there before the band set up, mostly to meet "The Duke." Only I kept falling asleep. Not unusual considering that I had none at all in the previous thirty-plus hours. I found it impossible to stay awake, and in self-defense, got dressed and walked around the row houses of old Philly for an hour or so. That was about all I saw of Philadelphia. I later came to realize that although I ended up visiting a lot of cities in a lot of states, I rarely got to see much more of any city than the area between the hotel and the concert venue, or the drive from the airport to the hotel. There was almost never any time for sight-seeing.

I got to the theater about an hour before time to open the doors, introduced myself to the ticket manager and his assistant, and headed back stage to meet Mr. Ellington and to explain that Irving wouldn't be there and that I would be handling the show that night if he needed anything. Duke's son, Mercer, was running around distributing the music parts, placing the charts on appropriate music stands, at the same time complaining loud enough for anyone to hear that he ought to be allowed to play with the band. Mercer played trumpet.

Every so often, he'd stop and ask Duke why he couldn't sit in on trumpet that night. Duke ignored him for awhile, but I guess he finally had enough. He took Mercer aside and set him straight, telling him that his job with the orchestra was as the band boy, at least for the time being. I had the distinct impression that Duke didn't particularly like his son, and for whatever reason, merely tolerated his presence.

Back in the box office, I watched the window sales like a hawk, but never saw anything that would lead me to suspect hanky-panky. I began to think I didn't know very much about that business, which was to a fairly large degree true, but I certainly didn't want the ticket manager to know that. If nothing else, I have always been reasonably adept at making people believe I knew things about which I actually knew little or nothing.

We weren't selling many tickets at the walk-in and I thought the audience would be pretty meager. Just before the first show started, I peeked through the peep-hole in the curtain and checked the house. It was far from empty. The difference would probably have passed unnoticed, at least by me, if I hadn't been looking for something. I just couldn't put my finger on anything specific.

At the break between shows, the ticket manager offered to take me to his close-by private club for dinner, an offer I readily accepted because finding any place to eat and have a drink in Philadelphia on Sunday was difficult. After a couple of drinks before dinner, I began to suspect that my host was trying to get me drunk, and I was sure it wasn't out of friendship. I could drink a lot in those days, and while I was feeling pretty good, I was far from intoxicated and I certainly had all my faculties working.

During dinner, I mentioned that it seemed to me there were more people in the auditorium than would seem possible considering the number of tickets still in the rack. He said it wasn't possible; that I must have been mistaken.

"Count the tickets for the second show when we get back," he said.

I answered that as it was my job, I would most certainly do that. Besides, I wasn't suggesting there was anything wrong in the ticket count, and of course, there wasn't. There were dollars for every ticket not in the rack.

Shortly after the doors opened for the second show, I noticed two couples going in, apparently without tickets. They handed the taker-taker a white piece of paper instead of the standard "pasteboards." I took a break and wandered into the lobby and over to the ticket taker. I asked to see what he had taken in lieu of tickets. He fished out two sheets of paper, each bearing the number and location of two seats.

"What the hell is this?" I asked. He explained that if someone lost their tickets, the box office would replace them with that "location" sheet. I took the paper into the box office and quickly found the tickets for those seat numbers still in the rack. It appeared that the ticket people were selling "locations" and pocketing the money. I issued orders to ticket takers to send anyone with a location sheet to the box office, which seemed to put an end to the stealing.

Flushed with success, I planned a relaxing, and I hoped, a sleep-filled trip, at least for the leg to Chicago, where I had to change airplanes, and Los Angeles. However, it was not to be. The people sitting behind me turned out to be the aunt and uncle of a high school chum; they insisted on talking to me about their nephew, Larry Fisher, who was then an attorney on his way to becoming a judge, all the way home. Except for the few minutes when I finally fell asleep during dessert.

CHAPTER THREE:
Talent Everywhere You Looked

Irving and I actually had two separate offices on the second floor at 451 North Canon Drive in Beverly Hills. There was a typewriter repair shop and Marshall Edson's Ye Little Club, a small bistro, on the ground floor. A talent agent, Alex Brewis, had the office between us. Alex represented a friend, Than Weyen, and so he and I had occasion to exchange small talk when Irving was out of town and I had done my work for the day. The best thing about Alex's office was his statuesque and gorgeous, cafe au lait-hued secretary, who had a "thing" for my company whenever Alex was out of town or when we both worked late.

Irving had one large office at the front of the building, overlooking Canon Drive; large enough to handle a seven-foot leather couch, his filing cabinets, a couple of chairs, and his desk. I had a smaller room immediately at the top of the stairs, which made me privy to everyone who came or went. A small office was fine with me because I could reach everything I needed simply by rolling my desk chair around. Of course, I did have to stand up to use the filing cabinet. Neither office could be described as "posh," but both were very functional. Irving's brother, jazz impresario, Norman, had offices at the end of the hall.

My office door was also directly across the hall from the management firm of (Ken) Kragen and (Ken) Fritz, and as I always kept my door open, visitors who didn't know better often thought I worked for them. As a result, I often interacted with their clients. Even after they learned who I was, their clients often stopped by my office first.

Kragen and Fritz were managing, among others, the Smothers Brothers, Pat Paulsen, singer/song writer/author Mason Williams, and The First Edition before it became *Kenny Rogers* and The First Edition, although Kenny was a member of the group at the outset. They also managed a couple of writers named Alan Bly and Bob Einstein, whose other writing partner in those days was writer/actor/comedian Steve Martin. Alan and Bob stopped at my office from time to time to show me original material they had written in addition to the scripts they were writing for *The Smothers Brothers Show.*

Mason Williams and I became friendly enough so that every time he wrote another book, he'd drop one off for me. Unfortunately, I never managed to get a Bus Book from him, and they are now worth beaucoup bucks. The Bus Book started out as a gag. Mason took a picture of a Greyhound Bus, had it enlarged in segments so that when each of the pictures was taped together it was equal in size to a real bus. He had the finished product mounted and set it up one night on a friend's front lawn. When the friend woke up, he saw what appeared to be a bus on his property. Mason had several copies made up. They folded into a hard cover, and he gave them away to friends. Unfortunately for me, they were very expensive to make and I wasn't that close a friend.

Mason told me that when he arrived in Los Angeles, he wanted to meet people, so he and a friend rented an antique or ultimate luxury, open car and parked it where there was lots of foot traffic. They sat in it or on it for a good part of the day and talked to people who stopped to look and ask questions.

Because the two Kens managed the Smothers Brothers, Irving was able to buy three dates, which we produced at the Pasadena Civic Auditorium. Everything went perfectly and all three, as I recall, sold out or nearly sold out. The two writers, Alan Bly and Bob Einstein went on to achieve even more fame, Alan as a writer and television producer, and Bob as Super Dave Osborne, among his many other accomplishments. Steve Martin achieved fame as a comedian, actor, and writer of considerable talent.

The First Edition, an immensely successful musical group even through several personnel changes, was created by a singer/songwriter named Mike Settle, and featured a very pretty and outstanding girl singer, Thelma Camacho. Kenny Rogers and Terry Williams made up the other members of the original group, all of whom came from The New Christy Minstrels. Mickey Jones, who had been with Trini Lopez, was asked to join them as the drummer. Mickey went on to become an actor in television and motion pictures.

PERKS AND HOW TO GET THEM

The two Kens also managed a duo called The Pair Extraordinaire. Marcus Hemphill played acoustic bass and Carl Craig, a terrific baritone, sang. That was it; just the two of them with no other musical accompaniment. They had a brief, but successful career, made a few records, and eventually went on to other things. I know that Carl often talked of going into television production, and I believe he did.

When I was in Columbus at the Ohio State Fair, I sold souvenir books for the headliners, Andy Williams and Henry Mancini. I read that Marcus and Carl were appearing at The Bistro, a favorite hangout for college students that was out on Olentangy River Road. Andy and Henry were featuring a new opening act—a bunch of kids who called themselves The Osmond Family.

As long as I was going to be stuck in Columbus, Ohio for the week, I decided to visit Carl and Marcus and catch their show. I arrived to find a line of about a hundred people waiting to get in, and I wasn't about to become one of them. Marching to the head of the line, I summoned the club manager and informed him that I was from the Kragen and Fritz office, their managers, and was ushered directly back stage.

Because I had become friendly with Carl and Marcus back at the office, I was greeted warmly and asked to join them after the show at "some party," to which I heartily agreed. "Some party" turned out to be a fraternity bash off campus, near Ohio State University. Marcus and Craig were assured there would be lots of young girls and lots of beer. The party was one of those evenings where the degree of good time you had was measured by how much beer you consumed without actually throwing up. *Very "Joe College," and all very dull,* I thought.

Marcus and Craig were quickly surrounded by several white college girls, who I supposed were getting their jollies by showing each other just how liberal they were by hanging out with two black musicians. Marcus was sitting on a couch, each arm draped around a pretty, young girl, and both of them were falling all over themselves trying to out-nice one another. Marcus was certain he was going to get laid that night, but he didn't come close.

I was getting pretty bored, and I mentioned to an attractive and equally unimpressed young woman standing nearby that I thought college parties had lost a lot since I was of college age. On reflection, I was probably wrong. I suspect they were just as bad; I was just a lot younger. Like me, she was not drinking and like me, just watching what seemed to be a lot of forced merriment. I introduced myself and said that seeing how sick I could get wasn't really my idea of a wonderful time, and she agreed. I asked her why she was at this party for which she obviously had no taste and she explained that Jennifer, one of the girls with Marcus was a friend of hers.

Jennifer's father had died recently and Dolores promised to look after her and make sure she didn't get into any trouble. I said that was nice of her, and the conversation pretty much ended there.

I was just about ready to leave when Marcus asked if I wanted to join him and Jennifer for dinner before his show the next night.

"Wait a minute," I said, "let me see if I can get a date, too." I walked back to Dolores, the young lady with whom I'd been talking, and asked her if she would like to join me and her friend, Jennifer, and Marcus. She accepted, more I think to watch over her friend than because of my scintillating personality.

She also made it very clear that the date was for dinner, not for any sex or fooling around. That was fine with me, although if she had said she wanted to have sex with me, I probably wouldn't have turned her down. She was, after all, very pretty. The next night, the four of us went out early for Chinese food.

When we arrived at the restaurant, it was completely empty except for the manager, a couple of waiters folding napkins, and a bartender "arranging the olives in numerical order," to cop a line from actor Jim Backus. The owner took one look at us, one white guy, one black guy, and two young girls, and ushered us to the back of the restaurant in a corner, out of sight, in the event I suppose, that any other customers showed up.

I said to Marcus, "How did he know I was Jewish?"

He replied, "I guess he figures we've got to be trouble makers. You know what us Negroes are like when we get around white girls."

EVEN STARS NEED HELP NOW AND THEN

Andy and Henry finished their gig in Columbus and moved on to Cleveland, where I had been not too long before with The Beach Boys.

The hotel where we stayed back then featured a bar with live music, girls, and a dance floor. The Beach Boys and I naturally gravitated to the bar following the concert, particularly as there wasn't much else to do in Cleveland, other than visit a jazz joint in another hotel and getting cabs for us all hardly seemed worth the effort.

The Beach Boys were busy checking out what few unattached females were there, while I was sitting alone at the bar. I was approached by a man who just seemed to ooze Mafioso. I certainly didn't know what a gangster looked like, but it seemed to me that fellow would have been perfect type-casting as a gangster, or what I imagined one should look like. Later, I actually met a few and I was right. He would have fit right in.

Lenny L. was about five-foot-nine or five-foot-ten, and he wore pointed, black wing-tip shoes. His salt and pepper hair was combed straight back, with nary a hair out of place. His pearl-gray suit was obviously very expensive. As he approached, I thought of him as being sort of "square" in stature. Like a refrigerator. I fully expected him to say "dese" and dose" and to speak with an accent. He didn't. Neither was he particularly polished. He was, in fact, a real live gangster.

"You with those Beach guys?" he asked.

"Yes, I am," I replied.

"Lissen," he said, "if any of them want girls, just ask me; I run things around here. But don't wait too long to ask," he kind of chortled, "because I'm under a federal indictment."

"For anything in particular," I asked trying to seem interested and sympathetic.""Everything. You name it; they're trying to connect me with it."

"I'm sorry to hear that," I said. "When you say 'girls,' you mean prostitutes?"

"Yeah, they can have almost any dame in this room, except her," he pointed across the room to a sedately dressed, perfectly coifed, gorgeous blonde, whose face was familiar to me from the small parts she played in a good many movies. "She's mine."

"Well," I said, "I appreciate the offer, but they don't usually have any trouble getting girls. It's something they just seem able to do."

"Okay, I just thought I'd ask. I figger it's always nice to help out the celebrities if they got the urge."

He handed me his card, saying, "If you ever need me, gimme a call. If I'm not in the joint, I'll be glad to help."

The young publicist for the tour was a former basketball player from a small college. He was doing his first important job out of college as publicist for Andy Williams, and I suppose the tour in general. I hadn't thought much about Lenny until the young publicist asked if I knew any hookers for Andy and Henry in Cleveland. The reason he asked me was because he was from Cleveland, and very well-known there. Using pros eliminated the possibility of things like blackmail. Also, he didn't want it to get around that he needed professionals. After all, he had plenty of action for free when he was a star.

"Not personally," I told him, "but I know a guy. You can call him when you get in. He might remember me."

Of course, he made the call and asked Lenny to have two girls stop by his room for his approval before he sent them on to their eventual destination. Lenny dutifully sent the women to the young publicist's hotel door. He opened it, stared at one of the young ladies, whom, as it happened, turned out to be a girl he knew from his college days. If that last item wasn't entirely true, it did make a good story.

Chapter Four:
There Are Lessons to Be Learned

My first real tour with The Beach Boys, other than as a book seller, was barely longer than my one-night-stand in Kansas City. Once again, Irving had to leave the tour due to some personal emergency and I flew out to meet the group in Des Moines, Iowa. Once again, there was little for me to do other than start the show on time, and balance the box office when it was over. As an old friend lived in Des Moines, I invited him to the concert.

After the show, with nothing better to do in Des Moines, we returned to the motel, trailed by a horde of young girls, who in turn were being followed by a pack of young men. Somehow, everyone, including The Beach Boys, gravitated to my room, which was later to become almost a ritual. Since that was the first time I was totally in charge, I decided to be smart and check their drivers' licenses before I let anyone in, which turned out to be a good idea.

Half an hour later, thirty or so young people had jammed their way into my room, sprawling on the bed and the floor, sitting on whatever piece of furniture would accommodate them, or squeezed against one another standing. It was very cold outside, but the door was partly open, and a man came bursting in yelling, "Where's my daughter? She's only sixteen years old. If she's here, I'm calling the cops."

I invited the man to calm down and to come in and look around. "If she's in here, you'd better check her out because she's using a phony drivers' license," I said. Of course, she wasn't there, and I learned right there that if I was going to travel with The Beach Boys in the future, it would be a good idea to keep a close watch. I didn't want anyone in my charge ending up in some local pokey for statutory rape.

One other memory from Des Moines: I got up from the table in the coffee shop the next morning to pay the bill, and when I got back, someone had stolen my brand new topcoat.

We went from Des Moines to Davenport where we had to do two shows because the hall was so small. Unfortunately, I didn't have time to eat before the show, and when I finally had the box office settled and went out looking for an open eatery of some kind, it was too late. Actually, there was one place open, a real greasy spoon, crowded with young people and blue with cigarette smoke. I didn't bother to go in, but stopped on the street long enough to watch what appeared to be some sort of local mating ritual.

"Downtown" consisted of two one-way streets around which cars circled continuously. There were cars with boys and cars with girls, but no cars with boys *and* girls. That, I learned, was the regular, weekend get-together. Boys and girls yelled to one another from their cars in the hopes of making a connection. Once made, the two cars withdrew from the circle, paired off, and went about their business.

The next morning at breakfast, Dennis Wilson called me to his booth where he was sitting with a very pretty young lady. Dennis introduced me.

"Oh, I'm so happy to meet you," she gushed. "Dennis told me all about you."

I was immediately on my guard. "Oh? And what did he tell you about me?" I asked.

"He told me that you would get me a recording contract if I stayed with him last night."

"So how come you didn't stay with *me* last night," I asked, "if I'm the guy who's supposed to get you a contract?"

"Dennis said I had to stay with him because you're married."

"Right," I responded. "Do you have a demo record?" Unfortunately, she actually had one. "Why don't you just send it to the office and I'll see what I can do." It was a scene we played out more than a few times while I worked with The Beach Boys.

WILD DOINGS IN OKLAHOMA

From Davenport, we flew down to Tulsa, Oklahoma. It had been cold in Davenport, but it was colder in Tulsa, and I was still bitter about the loss of my brand new topcoat.

We arrived in the afternoon, giving me plenty of time to check the auditorium and have a leisurely dinner of with some of The Beach Boys at a nearby coffee shop. The temperature was down close to freezing when Carl Wilson, Mike Love, Bruce Johnston, and I left the restaurant to walk back to the hotel.

They were complaining about the cold, and I said, "This is nothing compared to winters in Chicago. When I was in the navy, stationed at Great Lakes, I would take walks bare-chested in weather worse than this." Of course, I was putting them on, but they called me on it.

Mike said, "I'll give you $50 if you can walk at this same pace all the way back to the hotel. No fast walking; no running."

Having been challenged, I had no choice but to take off my jacket and shirt, hand them over, and then walk the block back to the hotel and collect on the wager. He still owes me.

After the show the next night, Dennis wanted to go out and celebrate his twenty-first birthday. He wanted me to take him to a bar, where he could drink legally for the first time. Back in the late 1960s, Tulsa was a "dry" town. That didn't mean you couldn't drink; you just couldn't buy a drink at a bar. If you went out to a fancy dinner somewhere, you simply carried your bottle in a paper sack or something, and took it in with you. The bar, hotel, or dining room charged you a buck or more for the set-up, even a glass of water.

We returned to the hotel after the show because I had no idea where to find a bar, which in Tulsa would have been in a private club of some kind, or how to get admitted. I contacted the house detective—they actually had one—and asked if he could suggest a place we might go. His primary job that night was to keep girls from going up to The Beach Boys' floor, so I took him aside and said, "Now, we don't want trouble any more than you do, so if you see some girl trying to go upstairs, even if she's *with* one of The Beach Boys, you check with me first and I'll tell you if she's okay or not."

Oddly enough, he bought that, and in a matter of about twenty minutes, there were enough women on our floor to make for a good party and I could take Dennis out for his night on the town. The security man directed us to a place where he knew the owner and we could celebrate Dennis's coming of legal age, which was still twenty-one back then. He also managed to produce a bottle of vodka for us.

We drove to the bar, knocked on the door, identified ourselves through an honest-to-god peep-hole that was right out of the 1920s, and then we were admitted. Music was playing and half a dozen or so couples were on the dance floor, some with their dates and some with waitresses, all of whom were very good-looking, particularly in their abbreviated uniforms.

Dennis urged me to find out if anyone could ask a waitress to dance. The bartender explained that waitresses weren't required to do so, yet they could indeed dance with customers when the music was slow, but when it was up-tempo/disco, they danced alone, either on the floor or on tables. *Very nice*, I thought, and I conveyed the information to Dennis.

I gave our bottle to the bartender, who marked it with our names to insure that no one else drank from it. We had been sitting at the bar for about ten minutes when the bartender, probably not much over twenty-one himself, asked me about Dennis. I explained that he had just turned twenty-one a few days earlier and that we were celebrating his passage into manhood.

"I dunno," the bartender said. "He looks awful young to me."

"Well, he is young," I answered. "He's just twenty-one and that's pretty young to me."

"I think I ought to see some I.D. You know, just to be on the safe side."

I explained that Dennis did not normally carry an I.D. or even money, that he was still wearing the pants from his stage costume, and that his pants had no pockets, so even if he did carry an I.D., there was no place to put it. The bartender was still leery and suggested that we ought to leave. Dennis wanted to know what the problem was. I told him we were being thrown out and it didn't make any difference to the bartender that he was one of The Beach Boys.

I turned back to the bartender and asked, "What's the fine if he turns out to be under age?"

"$500."

"So, how about I give you $500 to hold until we leave, just in case some cop happens to walk in and gives you a ticket or something?" I was still carrying all the cash from the box office because I didn't want to leave it in my room, and there was no one around who could put it in the hotel safe, if indeed there was one.

Dennis said, "Give him $10,000."

I reached inside my jacket, took out $10,000, and then laid it on the bar.

"What the hell is that?" asked the bartender, as he jumped back away from the bundle of bills.

"$10, 000," I said. "Dennis said to give you $10,000. Just to hold, you understand; not to keep."

He wouldn't touch it. I'm sure he thought we had just knocked over a bank or something. He wouldn't relent, so I picked up the money, stuffed it back into my jacket pockets, and we reluctantly left the premises. Dennis was furious at being kicked out. He wanted me to call the police to have them come over and get us back in. I tried explaining that the police had better things to do than to come over and get him into a bar, particularly since he not only didn't have any I.D. with him and he didn't even have an I.D. back at the hotel.

After pretending to make a call to the cops from a nearby telephone booth, I convinced Dennis that we should return to the hotel, where I found our security friend and had him call the club to get us back in. Dennis really wanted to go back to dance with, and with luck, pick up a waitress with whom he had already gotten chummy. It never took Dennis very long to make a connection.

Less than ten minutes later, we were back at the club, and that time, we were welcomed with open arms by the owner, who arrived only moments after we left. He was very happy to have a famous Beach Boy there. Dennis autographed a place mat or something for him and went to sit at a table, where he could continue his pursuit of the waitress. The owner and I sat at the bar, killed our bottle, and then drank from his personal supply. I presumed the drinks were on him since I was paying for the set-ups at $1 or more a glass. When I finally settled up, I was presented for a bill for about $60. I guess it was the ice that made it expensive.

That was in 1966, and "long hair" meant down to the top of your collar. The Beatles had been called "long hairs" because their hair was kind of shaggy and covered their ears. Dennis' blond hair hung down to his shoulders.

The owner turned to me and said, "I think your friend may be in trouble."

"Why, what's he done now? I told him not to get fresh with any of the waitresses."

"No, he's being a good boy, but look over there." He pointed to a table with six guys, all around six-foot-three and 250 pounds, surrounding it, apparently making fun of Dennis and his hair. Dennis was not a person to avoid a fight. He was strong as a bull and fearless. He used to dive alone for Abalone in the middle of the night off Palos Verdes Peninsula in Los Angeles. He never thought about the dangers.

"What are you going to do if there's a fight?"

"Whaddya mean, what am *I* going to do?" I responded with as little panic as possible in my voice. "What are *you* going to do? This is your place, isn't it? You don't allow fighting in here, do you?"

"Well, not necessarily, but I don't intend getting between those monsters and your friend. I'll call the cops if something happens, but by then they may have laid some serious hurt on him. So . . . what are you going to do?"

"Christ," I said, "I guess I'll have to go help him; he's pretty valuable property and he's in my care." Now, by nature I am not a fighter. While not a devout coward, I have never gone out of my way to get into trouble, where Dennis, on the other hand, had never gone out of his way to avoid it.

"I think I'll just ignore it, and hope it just goes away."

I kept my eyes aimed either straight ahead or towards the owner, and silently prayed that nothing would happen. Well, nothing happened over the period of the next two drinks, so I took a chance and looked over at Dennis, who by then had the six bruisers sitting with him, apparently enjoying the heck out of one another. There were four waitresses hovering over them, and any problems seemed to have been settled amicably. I breathed a sigh of relief, which doubled when the behemoths finally excused themselves and left the bar.

I left my bar stool and went to sit with Dennis—to find out what happened—and not to take a crack at one of the several waitresses clustering around Dennis. *Why should he have all the fun?* I thought.

It seemed that those guys were the defensive line of a college football team in town for a game. They were out training on beer.

"Okay, Dennis, I said, "what happened? How come you got so chummy?"

"I just told them you were a black belt in karate and that if they started anything, you'd wipe up on them."

"Fuck," I said, "what if they decided to try me?"

"Well, I guess you would have gotten hurt."

I thanked him for his thoughtfulness and suggested that it was time for us to be leaving, too, particularly since Bruce Johnston had talked everyone into catching a 6:30 a.m. flight back to Los Angeles. He had to get back for a recording session and wanted company on the airplane.

Dennis didn't want to go back to the hotel alone. What he had in mind was a couple of waitress we'd been hustling. I asked the owner if he had any objection, and he replied that normally he wouldn't mind, but that they were short-handed that night and he really needed everyone to be there until closing.

"When's that?" I asked.

"When everyone goes home."

Since it appeared that no one was getting ready to go, I walked over to the door, locked it, and tried getting people to leave by telling them they ought to be in bed alone or with their date by that hour.

The owner asked, "What the hell are you doing?"

I said I was just trying to get people to go somewhere else and that I had locked the door to keep anyone else from coming in. He laughed and said, "Okay, take whoever you want and get the hell out of here."

NOT EVERYTHING GOES SMOOTHLY

At 6:30 the next morning, we were all on board the airplane, wondering if we would even get to take off. It was snowing in Tulsa and the ground was quickly freezing over, but the airline decided to chance it. The airplane accelerated on the runway, but then it fish-tailed as it gathered speed. It finally hit a snow and ice-free section, giving the airplane enough traction to get us air-borne. We were scheduled to stop in Oklahoma City, but that was canceled because of heavy snows, so we flew on to Dallas, where we were to have a two-hour layover.

Bruce kept saying, loud enough for anyone else in first class to hear, that our airplane was doomed and there was no way he was getting back on. I suggested that I might kill him because we were all there only because of him, but he was adamant, and even talked a few Japanese tourists into staying until the next day.

The rest of us continued home, while Bruce called a friend, Leighton Humphrey, Jr., who flew him back to Los Angeles the next day. Leighton's father was in the oil business, and Leighton, Jr. had his own airplane.

CHAPTER FIVE:
Flying for the Public Gets More Dangerous

In 1966, there was an air traffic controllers "slow down," a situation that our erstwhile President Reagan solved by firing them all. It took a couple of years before it was safe to fly again, and there was no way of insuring on-time arrivals at the various concert sites if The Beach Boys had to travel by regular commercial airlines. So, they chartered a DC-3 and a couple of pilots owned (well, the pilots weren't actually "owned"—just sort of rented) by famed race driver and car builder Carroll Shelby.

The tour started in Denver, but as there was no room on the airplane for me and 10,000 souvenir books, I went with them in a twin-engine Super Beechcraft chartered and paid for by The Beach Boys. You can be sure Irving wouldn't have paid for it. Ten minutes out of Los Angeles, the pilot asked if I was interested in learning his "world famous, six-minute instrument lesson." Needless to say, I was ecstatic about the idea as flying had always been a fantasy of mine, the only fantasy that didn't have the word "sex" attached to it. In no more than six minutes, no kidding, he showed me how to turn left and right, make a bank and turn, read the radio compass, the bank and turn indicator, and the altimeter, and pretty much how to avoid crashing into a mountain somewhere—as there are some serious mountains between Los Angeles and Las Vegas, which would be a refueling stop.

"Just watch your heading and when the airplane starts to drift off course, make the correction. Just be gentle with the controls and you won't have any problems."

Then, he left me alone and went to the back of the airplane to go to the john or whatever. I steered (I hesitate to use the word "piloted") the airplane to just outside of Las Vegas, where we had to land for refueling. When air currents first pushed the airplane up a few hundred feet or knocked it down about the same distance, I immediately pulled the nose up or pointed it down, which I soon discovered wasn't really necessary. If we went down, the next updraft pushed us back up. After a series of over-corrections, I got the hang of it and spent the rest of the flight to Vegas enjoying the view. It was there, in Vegas, where I made a very serious mistake.

FOOD FOR THOUGHT

After stopping long enough to refuel and for something to eat, which included some very gooey pineapple pie for me, I soon found I wasn't doing as well physically out of Las Vegas to Denver as I had from Los Angeles. We were flying above some very serious mountains and *really* bouncing all over the sky again, only worse. My stomach began to rebel.

Lots of sudden drops and just as sudden returns to original altitude were beginning to get to me. Still, I was holding my own, so to speak, with relatively moderate discomfort and queasiness until the pilot decided to eat the lunch he picked up in Las Vegas.

I even survived watching him eat a soggy, dripping tuna salad sandwich, but the melting chocolate donut did me in. I grabbed the bag from his lunch, gave back mine, and tossed it out the window, where it petrified somewhere in Zion National Park. Centuries from now, some paleontologist will discover it and wonder what life form it might have been.

After the Denver show, our roadies loaded the balance of the books into one of the equipment trucks they rented in Denver and I joined the group on the chartered DC-3 for the trip to St. Louis and then on to Kansas City again. That time, Irving had booked me into the Muhlbach Hotel in the heart of the downtown district, because, I suppose, it was close to the auditorium. I hate to think it was just because he was being cheap. It was one of the smallest hotel rooms I have ever seen. The one bed (a twin-size, not even a double) actually extended past the door molding, partly blocking the doorway, making it difficult to even enter the room. The bathroom was exactly three paces from the foot of the bed, which made it handy, but hardly comfortable.

I called down to the desk and asked for a change of room, but was told that Irving had specifically asked for the least expensive room for me. I told the desk clerk that I didn't much care what Irving wanted and I wasn't going to sleep there. They moved me to a room only slightly larger, but with a double bed that fit all the way inside the room.

After the concert, Dick Duryea, Road Manager for The Beach Boys, invited me back to their motel for the "usual" after show party. I explained that I was already in a hotel, my clothes were there, and that Irving wasn't about to pay for two rooms. Dick insisted, saying they would stop by the hotel in the morning and that if Irving was too cheap, The Beach Boys would gladly pay for the room. The truth of the matter was that they were most likely paying for the room at the Muhlbach, too, because Irving generally charged them for all of his and my travel expenses.

As it turned out, there was no party, but Dick had invited a young lady to meet him at his room. I was feeling pretty much like a fifth wheel, but Dick assured me that it was highly unlikely that anything was going to happen and there was always the possibility that we both might get lucky. The three of us had settled down on the floor for conversation and watching television, and we were contemplating the room service menu when there was a very loud knock on the door.

DENNIS THE MENACE—AGAIN

It was Dennis. He was lonely. The girl *he* brought back from the concert had done her job, or perhaps had *not* done her job, and she had been sent home in a taxi. He also knew Dick had a girl in his room, so naturally, Dennis wanted her, too. We kept telling Dennis to go away, that there was no girl in the room, but he wouldn't leave. Besides, as usual, he had ordered fried chicken and insisted that he wanted us to share it with us. Dick looked at me, I looked at Dick, and we agreed it was senseless to ignore him because Dennis was certainly not going to go away. It was either go to his room or deal with the distinct possibility that he might break the door down. The girl, naturally, stayed in Dennis's room when we finished eating.

ON THE ROAD AGAIN

Carroll Shelby provided two terrific pilots with his airplane. If there was ever any doubt about their abilities, and there wasn't, it would have been dispelled on our trip to Duluth, Minnesota. I was standing in the cockpit when the co-pilot informed me that there might be some problem ahead. The weather was worsening rapidly and there was already very little visibility at the airport. There was a definite possibility we might have to fly into Minneapolis and drive something more than 100 miles up to Duluth, which I really did not relish. If we had to drive, we wouldn't get into town until two or three o'clock in the morning.

The ride was already starting to get a little bumpy, and I was about to head back to the cabin to buckle myself down when the pilot suggested the possibility of flying above the storm at about 13,000 feet, but as DC-3s were not pressurized, the passengers might get a little uncomfortable. The pilots had oxygen for themselves so they wouldn't have any problems.

I asked, "What happens if we fly that high?" I was pretty sure of the answer.

He said, "You'll probably get light headed and maybe a little giddy."

I said, "Go ahead and do it. They'll never know the difference." I also suggested that we ought to go for Duluth if at all possible.

The pilots said, "What the hell, let's give it a try." I loved their attitude.

As we approached the field, there was no visibility at all. The "ceiling" was only 300 feet as we approached the airport, and dropping right with us as we descended. When we reached an altitude of just *under* 300 feet, we still couldn't see the ground. At 150 feet, there was still no sight of the field or runway. The pilots ordered us to sit down and hook up our seat belts, something we rarely had to do up until then. I left the cockpit, where I'd been watching our descent and the altimeter, and took my seat, too.

Looking out the windows, we saw nothing at all until we were at tree-top height—about forty feet above the ground, but they set the airplane down with not so much as a bump, and we broke into spontaneous and enthusiastic applause.

Following the concert, I called a restaurant I had been assured would still be open. They insisted that they were just about to close, but I was able to talk the owners into staying open a little longer for us, The Beach Boys, and the entire crew. The few people still in the restaurant finishing their meals recognized The Beach Boys, refused to leave, and wanted to join our party, which was just fine with us.

As we entered the restaurant, a trio was winding up a final set and several customers were dancing on the large dance floor. They were starting to pack up when Carl asked me to find out if the musicians would mind if he, Dennis, and Bruce Johnston jammed for a little while. It may have been because no one was in a rush to return to the dump of a motel where the promoter of the date had us booked. Encouraged by the remaining diners, the trio gave their approval, and for the next hour or so, the guys played music I never suspected them capable of while some of us danced with wives of the remaining customers.

One couple asked if anyone wanted to join them at an "Officers' Club" somewhere. As I was up for more dancing and not quite through drinking, and had *no* eyes for the dingy motel at all, I agreed to go along. Besides, the wife was a terrific dancer, and I thought that she was coming on to me. Her husband seemed to pay little attention to her and was drinking up a storm. I had the feeling he might be a little swish, or she was just trying to make him jealous, but what the heck, I was having a good time and saw no reason to stop. They invited me to stay at their home for the few remaining hours until we had to leave, and I agreed, just as long as they got me to the airport on time.

At their home, we had a few more drinks. I sat on the floor, and the wife lay on the couch behind me, wearing only a diaphanous peignoir, and the husband eventually passing out cold on a chair across the room. I'm reasonably certain I did not sleep with the wife, although I seem to recall her encouraging a little groping on my part at least. I *know* I did not sleep with the husband—I suspect one doesn't forget that kind of experience—and somehow I ended up sleeping on a cot in the basement recreation room. The next morning, I was awakened by a very surprised baby sitter when she came into the house through the basement and said, "Who the hell are you?"

Our next two stops were Fargo and Minot, North Dakota. Needless to say, there was nothing to do in either town after the performance. We were lucky to find anything to eat, let alone anyone to party with. In Minot, Alan Jardine and I stood in the hotel parking lot, waiting for *Sputnik*, the Russian satellite, to fly by. After fifteen or twenty minutes, we noticed *Sputnik* appear as a bright spot moving across the heavens, and we stood transfixed on that tiny dot of light sailing past us. We watched until it vanished from sight, and then we returned to our rooms. So much for Minot, North Dakota.

The next two dates were at Victoria and Vancouver, British Columbia. The hotel in Victoria had a health club on the top floor, and Dennis got permission to use it after the concert. Normally, it would have been closed at that hour, but they were kind enough to keep it open just for us.

The steam room was very large and equipped with showers and benches in several locations. I had never seen anything like it. It easily accommodated our entire entourage, plus the several females Dennis managed to recruit. I found myself playing checkers with Bruce.

The next night in Vancouver, the book sales went very well. I put the cash—about $300—in my attaché case and left it in the theater office for safe-keeping until it was time to go back to the hotel. When I came back for the case, I found that the money had been stolen. I felt terrible, mostly because Irving would expect me to make up the loss; a loss I could hardly afford on my salary.

A CURE FOR THE BLUES

We had to charter an airplane to carry the equipment because some of the jumps across Canada were too far to drive. I was moping around the hotel when one of the cargo airplane pilots found me. He had a date with a cocktail waitress at Isy's Supper Club, one of

Vancouver's better-known night spots, and insisted I come along with him.

Susan Gibson, the young lady in question, was still working in the second floor "Roaring Twenties Room" when we got there. We had a drink, and because she was going to be tied up for another half-hour or so, we went downstairs to catch the show in the main room.

Isy's was home to the top acts of Canada and the United States during its day. Just about every major act played there over the years. Isy Walters and his brother, Richard, owned two clubs, the second being The Cave, but Isy's had semi-nude Las Vegas-style showgirls all taller than five-foot ten, specialty acts, and a complete revue. One of the bouncers and I got friendly, and he and his girlfriend, one of the showgirls, decided to join us after closing.

Susan led us to another club with music and dancing, and when she heard what happened to me, insisted on trying to cheer me up by dragging me onto the dance floor where I taught her to Bossa Nova. We must have made an interesting sight; me just a tad over six feet and she barely five feet tall. No one in the party would give me any time to think about how miserable I was, and so I made it through the night in reasonable shape.

WE BECOME FAMOUS AMONG RECORD PEOPLE

From Vancouver, we flew down to Spokane, Washington, where the promoter had booked us and The Pickle Brothers into a Holiday Inn. The genesis of The Pickle Brothers' comedy act had been in another comedy group, the Ace Trucking Company. That particular Holiday Inn was more like a resort than a typical Holiday Inn; more motel than hotel. Several one-story structures enclosed a huge grass area and a pool.

The disc jockey at the station that promoted our gig arranged dinner dates for me and Dick Duryea. Dick decided he wasn't interested, but one of The Pickle Brothers, Ron Prince, offered to replace him.

Digressing for a moment to a time perhaps three years later, I was introduced to a young man from Vanguard Records and I learned that we were famous.

He said, "Oh, I know all about you."

"From where?" I asked.

"Room 108, Holiday Inn, Spokane, Washington." He said.

I was momentarily taken aback, and then I asked him, "Were *you* there?"

He replied, "No, but you guys are a legend in Spokane."

I said, "Not me. How the hell did my name get involved? I *was* there, but I was the only one who didn't actually take part. Well, I and one other guy, but he didn't count."

What happened was that after dinner, my date and I stopped at my room, where I poured us each a drink from the bottle I usually carried on tour.

While we were having our drink, Linda, whose husband was overseas in the armed services, asked, "Do you like water sports?"

I answered, "Well, I swim a little, but I'm not into other . . . ." I suddenly realized that she was not referring to *that* kind of sporting activity at all. I started to say something, but she interrupted.

"Never mind," she said. "Too late. Forget I asked."

I knew right then I blew whatever chance there was that my evening might have been extended. Well, that's not exactly true. It *could* have been extended, but I preferred otherwise under the circumstances that presented themselves a few moments later.

I was rescued from my embarrassment by a telephone call from Ron Prince, who was the tenant of what was to become the infamous room 108. "We're having a party," he said. "Would you mind lending us your date? Of course, you're invited, too."

I replied, "I'm not in any position to lend her to anyone. I'll ask her if she wants to join your party, but why?"

It seemed that there were sixteen men in room 108, and only one girl, Linda's girl friend, "Sally." I have no idea what her real name was, so that name will do. "Sally" was doing her best to sexually satisfy all of them. Unfortunately, she just couldn't handle the crowd and asked for help. I turned to Linda and explained the situation, asking if she would like to join her friend. She said, "Well, I've never done anything like that, but I wouldn't mind going to have a look."

We walked into the room, which was pretty much packed with naked men and one naked lady, actively engaged in a heroic effort to service three of them, Carl Wilson and two band members, at once. There was one man, other than myself, still clothed; the leader of the band we were carrying with us. He was obviously agitated, which was understandable because he was gay. I have no idea why he was there unless he just liked looking at naked guys. He certainly wasn't going to get any action. One of The Beach Boys asked me to introduce him to Linda, which I did.

He said to me, "Do you mind if I fuck her?"

I replied once again that I had nothing whatever to say about it, and that he was strictly on his own, although I would introduce him, which I did. I didn't mention anything about "water sports."

Never having been one interested in group nakedness or group sex, I excused myself, coping out by explaining that I had to be up early the following morning to get the show on the road. Not that anyone cared much what I did or said at that point, just as long as I left Linda.

I learned nothing of the rest of the night until the following morning, when "Sally" came into my room and asked if she could hide out for a little while. I say she "came into my room," which is accurate. I had not quite closed the door when I returned from room 108, and she just walked right in. As it was nearly time for me to get started for the trip to the airport, I was already awake. She crawled into my bed—fully dressed—and certainly in no mood for any additional sex. The clear alternative was for me to get dressed and head for the coffee shop, stopping only long enough for her to tell me of the night's events.

She explained that around six o'clock in the morning, most of the men decided to go swimming—a fact I was well aware of from the noise they were making—which is why I was awake when she came in. She chose that time to get dressed and escape. It seems that she and Linda did indeed take on all sixteen of them. She was completely worn out and said that she had never even been with two men before.

I asked whether or not she enjoyed herself, and she admitted that until total exhaustion set in, she was indeed having a good time. "I don't think I'll ever do it again, though," she said. Linda, it seems had gone swimming with the guys and apparently was to meet her girl friend a little later. I finished my packing, went to the coffee shop, had breakfast sent to each of The Beach Boys, and got ready for the next leg of the trip to Boise, Idaho.

Once I was back at the office, I actually heard from Linda. She dropped me a note to tell me that her husband was coming back from the service and that she hoped I would never mention her by name just in case the details of the orgy in room 108 ever got back to Spokane. Of course, Linda is not her right name. At least, I think it's not her right name.

SIGHT-SEEING THE HARD WAY

From Boise, we flew on home to Los Angeles, but not without a side trip. By that time, I was on very friendly terms with our pilots, who were enjoying the trip as much as anyone. Generally, when flying Carroll Shelby around, they had to be on their best behavior, but that trip was different because we invited them to take part in anything we did. As a rule, though, they went off by themselves and found their own entertainment.

In one city, I found them sitting in the lobby of our hotel around two o'clock in the morning, each with their arms around two extremely unattractive women. I wondered how they managed to find four such uglies in one place. You'd think that two good-looking pilots would have done better. In their state of inebriation, I'm sure all four of them looked beautiful.

A comedian friend explained it this way: "I like to start early and drink 'em pretty." Neither pilot could stand on their own, but the four women with them were more than up to the task and eager to help them to their respective rooms. Amazingly, by eight o'clock the next morning, they were at the airport, lunch boxes loaded on board, and ready to fly, which was a testament to the efficacy of oxygen, I guess.

After we were airborne, one the pilots asked over the intercom whether anyone wanted to fly the airplane. Having had my six-minute instrument lesson, I felt ready for bigger stuff, as long as I didn't have to take off or land. Dennis wanted to try it, too, but all he did was get into the co-pilot's seat and sit there. Finally, I told him to either do something or get out of the way. He got out of the way.

I crawled into the seat, buckled myself in, and looked at the myriad of instruments, which were many more than on the Super Beechcraft. I asked, "Does this fly just like a Beechcraft?" Assured that it did, I located the radio compass, the bank and turn indicator, and the altimeter, and made a couple of tentative turns to the right and left. Then, I put it into a reasonably steep bank to the left and then the right, which seemed to shake up the boys in the back, and flew towards Los Angeles for half an hour or so. I decided that flying, once I was up there, was for me. Getting up and down was quite another matter.

The pilot finally took over the controls and asked if I had ever been to Yosemite National Park. When I said I hadn't, he asked if I would like to see it up close. Of course, I wanted to. He radioed a change of flight plan and headed for the park.

My memory might be a little hazy, especially as I still haven't seen Yosemite from the ground, but this is the way we saw the place:

We flew in low over what appeared to be a lodge or resort, set on a point of land high above the valley floor. We passed a hundred feet or so above the parking lot and headed towards the large face of a cliff that the pilot identified as Half Dome. Then, he put the airplane into a sharp left bank towards Bridal Veil Falls, from which very little water was cascading. More like a drip than a cascade. As we neared the falls, we made another sharp left bank and dropped quickly down into the canyon. We flew past El Capitan, an almost perfectly perpendicular wall of granite down which sky divers loved to jump and up which rock climbers like to climb, then along the length of the canyon. Presumably at a point where it would have no longer been safe to continue, we returned to normal altitude for the remainder of the trip home.

CHAPTER SIX:
They Got Each Other, Babe

I don't want to convey the impression that all I did was travel. Quite the contrary, I spent most of my time in the office doing the things Irving rarely did before I got there, like keeping records, paying bills (he did pay bills, but frequently only after being dunned), writing and placing publicity, and redesigning newspaper ads. Irving liked stars on his ads—they were all over his ads; they were cluttered with stars. I kept some stars, but designed ads that, as we said in advertising classes at USC, "sold."

For the most part, when I traveled, it was with Irving for the purpose of selling souvenir books. Irving liked being on the road, partly because it kept him out of his home and away from his wife, with whom he was usually feuding and partly because he pretty much lived it up on the road. When they married, he lived in his own apartment for a few months because, as he said, "this isn't one of those things you just jump into."

Irving also produced concerts with Jimi Hendrix, The Rolling Stones, Sonny and Cher, Paul Revere and The Raiders, Chad and Jeremy (the latter two on *their* money), Nancy Wilson, The Smothers Brothers, The Kingston Trio, Peter, Paul and Mary, Jonathan Winters, Bill Cosby, Shelly Berman, Ella Fitzgerald (his first concert on his own), some jazz shows, Latin music shows, and too many others to recall. Obviously, he didn't have to rely on The Beach Boys for the bulk of his income. They represented extra cash. By the time I joined Irving in 1965, he was already successful.

In addition to concerts, Irving contracted to produce souvenir books for several acts and sold them on the road and locally, giving a percentage to the act. There was more than enough work to keep us both busy. When he was in the office, Irving spent most of his time on the telephone making deals with agents, and when buying acts, calling newspapers and radio stations to determine who was "hot" in whatever area he was doing a show. I did all the follow-up work and was actively learning the business, and figuring out what Irving did that I would or wouldn't do, were I in charge.

I realize that the following anecdote is out of chronological order, but it sort of fits here: on one of the tours I worked, other than The Beach Boys, and even then not the entire tour, was for Sonny and Cher, whom Irving had hired for *The Beach Boys Summer Spectacular.* They were very easy to work with and truly nice people, so when they asked Irving to produce a tour for them, he accepted. Besides, like The Beach Boys, they would pay for it.

At that time, Sonny and Cher lived in a home high in the hills above Encino, California. From their patio, which was really a cantilevered deck, you could see a beautiful view of most of the San Fernando Valley. My family and I lived in Encino, too, but on the flat land "north of the boulevard." "South of the boulevard" meant you had money or were living beyond your means.

One night, I had to drive up the hill to their home to talk to Sonny about the tour. I took my son, daughter, and my daughter's girlfriend along for the ride, just so they could say they saw where Sonny and Cher lived. When Cher learned they were outside in the car, she went out and got them, gave them a tour of the house and grounds, and fed them cookies and milk. She was a really good kid and I liked her a lot.

We did a concert with them in Bakersfield, which I recall as being on New Year's Eve. I remember Irving and me driving in a hurry back to the San Fernando Valley, exactly 100 miles from my house, because we were late for a party. The concert was a huge success. The Civic Auditorium was brand new and the facilities state-of-the-art, especially for the 1960s. The theater held about 3,000 people with perhaps twenty feet of open space between the front row and the edge of the stage, which was elevated only about six inches. The slope of the auditorium was steep so everyone could see, even with the low rise of the stage.

Cher was very timid in those days and was worried about being so close to the audience. She had a fear of being mauled by her fans, which was maybe not so unreasonable considering the way everyone wanted to get close to and perhaps even touch her. Even then, Cher was the real star of the act and Sonny was smart enough to know it. We had to hire extra security people just to make her comfortable.

For a concert in San Diego with them, I parked a car inside the auditorium at a side entrance in the hopes that we could make our escape before their fans could figure out that we had left the building. It took us perhaps only two minutes too long, and by the time I tried to drive out of the building, about 200 youngsters had the car surrounded, pounding on the hood, top, and fenders. It was, I suppose, their way of expressing their love. To Cher, it was a nightmare, as she cowered in the back seat until I managed to force my way through the crowd.

On the tour, we played venues including Davenport, Iowa, Cleveland, Ohio, and Detroit, Michigan. I caught an early flight after the Cleveland concert, leaving Sonny and Cher to follow leisurely. Besides, they were not early risers, and we had a couple of free days before the show.

DETROIT—WE HAVE A PROBLEM

For some reason, ticket sales were not booming. As soon as I checked into the Ponchartrain Hotel, I called newspaper editors at the *Free Press* and the *Detroit News*, and some radio people to find out what was wrong. As hot as they were, Sonny and Cher should have been an easy sell out.

I learned that audiences were wary because Sonny and Cher had apparently failed to show at the same auditorium six or seven months earlier and there was little or no money left in the box offices for refunds. No one had bothered mentioning the problem to us when we were booking the date.

The truth of the matter was that a promoter advertised the date, made deals with a radio station and newspapers, arranged for the box office and ticket sales, and then made periodic "raids" on funds, supposedly to cover media bills, a practice not uncommon back then.

There was only one problem: no one told Sonny and Cher about the date and they had never signed any contracts with anyone. When they failed to show up, the public blamed them. The unscrupulous promoter had, by then, gone "south" with most of the receipts.

I did some radio and newspaper interviews to deny that Sonny and Cher had anything to do with the scam and to assure the public that they would indeed be there. As soon as they arrived in town, I arranged interviews for them and spent a few dollars more for air time. We salvaged the show as they say, "in the nick of time."

Once again, Irving had to stay in Los Angeles because of some personal business, but he caught up with us in Detroit, arriving in time for the concert, after which I returned to Los Angeles while he finished the tour, I think in Texas.

FINDING AN UNDERSTANDING IN-LAW

Going to Detroit had special meaning for me because I got to meet my brother-in-law, his wife, and their children for the first time. I had no inkling of the type of person Norman Wexler was other than what my wife, Phyllis, had told me. He was an artist, sculptor, and a designer and creator of jewelry, an early bohemian, who ran away from home when he was sixteen. Phyllis and I had been in Detroit for a few days back in 1953, and I had met most everyone other than Norman.

I met Norman at the used bookstore he owned out near Wayne State University. It took about two minutes for us to become friends. "What are you doing tonight?" he asked.

"Nothing. I don't know anyone else here except some of your relatives and I don't really have time to see them."

"I promise they'll never know you were here. You want to go to a party tonight?"

"Sure," I said, "why not?"

"Do you want a little grass?"

"Sorry, don't use it. I'm not into anything except alcohol."

"Hey, that's okay with me. You want to get laid?"

I thought that was very friendly for a brother-in-law I just met.

"Don't go to any trouble for me," I said. "But a date for the party would be nice."

"No problem. I'll have a girl for you at the party and you can drive her home. What you guys do is between you two."

That's what I call the perfect brother-in-law.

SOMETIMES, YOU GET TO SELECT YOUR SEAT MATE

Sonny made the most of their visit by inviting a dozen or so members of his family to dinner at the hotel. It turned into a three-hour feast. When I returned to Los Angeles the day after the concert, I had to purchase an extra, first class seat on the airplane for a six-foot-tall, stuffed doll for their daughter, Chastity. The doll got the window seat. Later, I did much the same thing for Mike Love of The Beach Boys. Not with a doll, but with a buttermilk churn he found when we were driving through the Blue Ridge Mountains.

THE ENGLISH INVADE

I ended up in St. Louis again when Irving purchased a few dates with Peter Noone and his band, better known as Herman's Hermits. Peter was one of the nicer people I met in the rock and roll business, although there were more than a few good ones. There were also a few not so good ones.

We played The Opera House, which was part of a huge building, the "theater" section of which occupied considerably less than half, the balance of which was devoted to "The Arena." In order for us to rent the hall, we had to share the building as the Arena was already booked for wrestling, which meant there was a smaller stage for us to use. It made no difference to us as we had no need for depth. We had to, as they described it, "play in front of the steel," which was the fireproof "curtain" used to separate the two portions of the building.

We discovered that it was possible to walk around to the other side of the steel curtain and watch the wrestlers, albeit from a considerable distance. While the opening act was busy opening, Peter and I and some of the band members watched the wrestlers.

While we were standing there, two women wrestlers worked their way over to see what was going on in The Opera House. Two band members were immediately taken with the ladies (you know them kinky English) and made dates for that night. They were absolutely certain they were going to get laid, and they may have. The ladies were very taken with their English accents, which they thought were "cute."

ONE OF THE NOT SO NICE

Irving decided to book three concert dates with a hot young singer/pianist/song-writer named Janis Ian, splitting the dates, costs, and profits with another promoter. We scheduled performances in Fresno and a couple of other middle California cities, the names of which have escaped me. It was in Fresno, the first of the three dates, which provided a memory of one of the "not so nice performers."

We hired an up-and-coming young band as an opening act. They had one record that was beginning to make some noise on the charts, and we thought it might attract a few more people. Janis was a quiet, acoustic act, playing piano for herself. The opening act was just the opposite—hard rockers.

I went to the auditorium early, as was my practice, to check on the stage set-up, lighting, sound, ticket sales, and all the dozens of little things that go with producing a concert. Irving was going to fly up that night and do the remaining dates.

When I walked into the hall, the first thing I noticed were fourteen double-stacked columns of powerful Marshall speakers and amplifiers taking up the entire back of the stage. As Janis was basically an acoustic act with some amplified accompaniment, I knew they were not hers. I also noticed that there was no room to set up her band's amps and speakers. The opening act was just finishing their rehearsal and I thought they sounded pretty good, although in the small auditorium we were using, they hardly needed all that sound equipment.

I approached the leader, identified myself, and asked politely, "Jim, would you mind taking down a couple of those columns so Janis has room for her stuff?"

He told me, in language I hardly expected from someone I just met, to "go fuck yourself." I did my best to be polite in spite of his attitude, figuring the guy was just an asshole.

I tried to explain that he really wouldn't need all that power considering the size of the facility and that removing two amps and speakers could hardly make much of a difference. Then, he really got mad.

"Why the fuck aren't we the headliners, and why the fuck aren't we getting more money?" he screamed.

Considering that I was obviously talking to a dangerous lunatic, I pointed out as best I could that Janis was the #1 act in the country at that moment and that I was sure his time would come. In the meantime, I asked why he couldn't be a little more cooperative. That, too, failed to set well with him. By then, I was getting a little more than perturbed and told him so. I suggested that if he didn't arrange to remove a couple of columns I would have it done for him.

At that moment, Ray Manzarek, Jim Morrison's keyboardist, intervened and actually stood between us, to keep me from getting killed, I suppose, and told me that he would take care of it personally. I was about ready to call my interview with the leader of The Doors closed when he did one more thing that upset me.

A man about eighty years old was busy sweeping up in front of the stage in preparation for the evening. Just after he finished the front area, Morrison took a box of popcorn and threw it on the floor behind him. I questioned the reason for his doing that unkind act and suggested that he get his ass off the stage, apologize to the old man, and then sweep it up himself. He flew into an absolute rage and headed for me. Considering that I did not enjoy physical confrontation, I was *almost* looking forward to it. Little did I know how strong and how insane he was. Once again, Ray Manzarek stepped in between us, grabbed Morrison, and shoved him away. He again apologized for Morrison's actions and jumped down from the stage to talk to the old man. Needless to say, that was the end of my relationship with Jim Morrison. I was happy to return to Los Angeles when Irving got there.

CHAPTER SEVEN:
We Go Big Time Again

The first really big event for Irving in 1966 was *The Beach Boys Summer Spectacular* at the Hollywood Bowl, which I have mentioned earlier. We followed a week later at the San Francisco Cow Palace, named incidentally, for the fact that it was used largely for livestock shows before promoters got around to using it for concerts.

Irving talked The Beach Boys into the Hollywood Bowl event in 1965, and because it was moderately successful, they were anxious to do it again in 1966, primarily because they earned some positive publicity in Los Angeles. Oddly enough, while they were a giant act throughout the world, they were not nearly as popular in their own home town. They were always a huge draw almost everywhere else in this country, and even more so in Europe and Japan.

In England, they played before hundreds of thousands of screaming, adoring fans, a crowd estimated at a 500,000 in Hyde Park, but in Los Angeles they couldn't, as the saying goes, "draw flies." The idea of The Beach Boys headlining a concert with perhaps fifteen of the top acts in the country was again very appealing to them, even if they did have to front the expense money.

The Bowl was one of the more expensive venues in the country. We had to start with a deposit of $9,000. As I recall, we scaled the house to an average cost per ticket of around $4, unbelievably low in terms of where the cost of acts escalated only a few years later. With some 17,000 seats, our gross would then have been in the neighborhood of $68,000; not a lot of money by 1990's standards, but very good when you consider the fact that we paid the #1 act in America only $4,000.

We held back perhaps a hundred seats for media, personal comps, and VIPs. Even taking into consideration all the freebies, with a near sell out everyone still would have done pretty well, especially Irving, who would get his usual 10 percent off the top.

We had no problem in securing the cooperation of a radio station as a sponsor, but spent considerable money in newspaper advertising. However, as time grew shorter, we were a long way from selling out. Considering the number and caliber of the acts we hired, we could not imagine anything less than a full house.

Irving and I did a lot of brain-storming and I suggested we might hire an airplane to fly the beaches towing a banner advertising the show. Irving added the thought that we should go to the beach that same day and hand out fliers. We took twenty or thirty sets of tickets down to Santa Monica and recruited youngsters to put handbills on every blanket on the beach. We covered the beaches from Santa Monica to Zuma, passing out several thousand fliers. Then Irving had a hundred or so posters printed, and although it was strictly illegal, we went out at night and tacked them up on most of the telephone poles in Hollywood and along the Sunset Strip.

I no longer remember every act on the bill, but I do remember some of them. Among them were the English folk music duo Chad and Jeremy, who got about $400. We also booked Percy Sledge, who had the #1 record in the country at the time, "When a Man Loves a Woman." He got around $750. Sir Douglas (Doug Sahm), Captain Beefheart, and Dino, Desi, and Billy, who were paid $150 because we thought the kids were worth $50 each. The Byrds were paid in the neighborhood of $1,500, while the new, hot kid who sat on a stool dressed all in black, accompanying himself on guitar— Neil Diamond—got $100. The highest-paid act on the show was the #1 concert/recording act in the country at the time: The Lovin' Spoonful.

WE BECOME SORT OF MATCHMAKERS

I mentioned that The Byrds were part of the show, and that brings to mind a story about of couple of their groupies. One day, the telephone rang in our office and the girl on the other end of the line said, "My girl friend and I go to every Byrds concert, no matter where it is."

I said, "That's very nice. I'm sure they appreciate it. What can I do for you?"

"We want to buy tickets," she said.

"Well, there are still lots of them available. You can pick them up at the box office."

"That's the problem," she said. "We're still in Chicago and we want the best seats we can buy, so will you save us two seats and we'll come to your office next week and pay you."

I agreed to do it, and when Irving came back to the office, I told him what happened. We figured we might be able to get a nice bit of publicity out of the story, which we did. The *Los Angeles Times* picked up the story and ran a feature with their picture.

The girls were both from wealthy families, who didn't seem to mind terribly that their teen-age children chased a rock and roll group around the country, and kept financing their travels.

One girl was so desperately thin that the go-go boots she wore never touched her calves. The other was as chunky as her friend was skinny. She wore dead-white makeup that made her look like a fat cadaver. Their dream was to have sex with every member of the band, and they wanted to know if we could help.

"Have you had any luck so far?" I asked.

"No, but then we've never had enough time before. We're staying in town for awhile because they're going to be here."

"Look," I said, "we can tell them how you feel and I'd be happy to give them your telephone number here, but the rest is up to them."

The girls were more than satisfied and were eventually successful to some degree. They decided to stay in Los Angeles for a few more weeks and called to say that they had been at least partially successful in their quest with The Byrds. However, they had another project in mind. They came to the office with a list of local rock musicians they wanted to bed down, and they again asked for our help.

I explained that as I was not a pimp, it was not something I wanted to do, but they begged and I felt a little sorry for them. What I did was let as many of the names on their list know about the girls, gave out their telephone number at a motel on the Sunset Strip, and left the rest to them. After four or five months of chasing their Los Angeles dream, they finally took off after The Byrds again.

THINGS GET SETTLED IN HOLLYWOOD

The Hollywood Bowl employed Gordon Jenkins, Jr., son of the famous conductor/arranger, as their sound engineer; one of the two or three best I have ever worked with. He placed microphones at all the amplifiers so he could control the balance between voices and music. We utilized the Bowl's revolving stage to move acts on and off quickly. Because Gordon had achieved such a remarkable balance of sound, always difficult at the Bowl except for symphony orchestras, we told each act not to touch their amplifiers nor change the amp volumes under any circumstances because they would screw up the sound.

Ordinarily, rock acts would crank up the volume so they could, as they insisted, hear themselves better when they were singing. However, we had more than enough monitors on stage for them and there was really no reason to make changes other than from force of habit.

Chad and Jeremy, with young Jim Guercio as their lead guitarist, did as they were told and were the hit of the first half of the show. Jim Guercio later became one of rock music's premier entrepreneurs with groups like Chicago and The Mob. He later moved to Colorado, bought a ranch, and opened a recording studio while continuing to manage and produce. Jimmy was a movie buff, and he could tell you things about almost every movie that came out during his youth. His father was a motion picture projectionist in Chicago and Jim saw everything . . . many times.

While we were setting the revolving stage for The Lovin' Spoonful, Dick Duryea and I cautioned their Road Manager not to touch the amplifier settings. He said he would if he wanted to, and if the musicians wanted to make changes on stage, he would tell them they could.

Dick suggested that if he didn't tell them not to touch their amps, we would push the button on the revolving stage and take them right off, even in the middle of a song. Their Road Manager complained that we couldn't do that because his group was the most important in the country. We said, "Yeah, try us." Not only that, we weren't going to pay them if they don't play. I doubt seriously that Irving had any idea what was going on back stage.

Things were much different in the music business then. Promoters had some say-so in the way their concerts were conducted. It wasn't until a few years later that fringe promoters and the acts took control and prices got out of hand. A lot of independent promoters, like Irving, bit the bullet and just quit the business. Irving continued doing some events, I believe in conjunction with Lou Robin and Alan Tinkley, for whom we had produced some Bill Cosby dates.

While The Lovin' Spoonful didn't tamper with their amplifiers, The Beach Boys did. Dick solved that problem when he walked out onto the stage while they were performing and turned their amplifiers down, cautioning them, "Don't ever do that again." They left everything alone after that, and in the end, it came off wonderfully.

We took most of the same show to San Francisco and added Country Joe McDonald and The Fish, Grace Slick and The Jefferson Airplane, The Grateful Dead, and a new "surf group," The Sun Rays, managed by Murry Wilson, father of Brian, Dennis, and Carl, and uncle of Mike Love of The Beach Boys.

Murry took me aside and asked me to give them a better position on the show. "I'll give you a bottle of good scotch, if you do," he said. I replied that I didn't drink scotch, and that the decision would have to be left to The Beach Boys. While they no longer had much to do with Murry, and in fact pretty much disliked him, they still approved the change. It made very little difference because the audience didn't pay much attention to them anyway.

Country Joe's manager informed me that we could expect "anything" from his act.

"Like what?" I asked.

"Well," his manager said, "he's been known to urinate on stage."

"Not on our show he won't," I said.

"He will if he wants to, because he's into making statements."

I suggested, "That is one statement he won't make here if you want to get paid." There was considerable posturing and moaning and groaning, but in the end, they behaved themselves.

I met someone else backstage at the Cow Palace. I'm not even sure how he got back there, but as I came to know Steve Tolin better, I realized that if he wanted to be somewhere, he got there. For some reason, he had decided I was the man to talk with, not Irving. Steve managed a young singer named Johnny Draper, then working as the lead singer in a group called The Cheaters, and for some reason he wanted my help in promoting him. I told him that I only "worked here" and most likely wasn't in a position to help him, but he insisted I come to hear his young protégé after the show. Johnny was the son of a then very well-known country singer, Rusty Draper, and Steve thought that fact alone might help promote the young man's career. In the end, it didn't work out.

I agreed to go hear his singer, mostly to keep Steve off my back, and once everything was wound up for the night, went with him in his car to a club somewhere in San Francisco. That was my initial mistake. I had no idea where he was taking me and I had no idea until we got there that Johnny didn't go on until after two o'clock in the morning. It seems that this club was strictly "after hours." Well, I was stuck and there was nothing I could do about it, so I listened, told Steve I thought the young man had some talent, and that I had no idea how to help him.

CHAPTER EIGHT:
Paul Revere: Not the Patriot

As time went on, Irving realized he couldn't possibly be at every concert with every act, so he sent me out to handle dates he wasn't particularly interested in working. One of those short tours was with Paul Revere and the Raiders.

Paul, a barber from Boise, Idaho, was a very shrewd businessman. He created the idea of an "All-American" group, clean cut, but not in any way like The Beach Boys; more straight rock and roll. He had gotten very popular, and his lead singer, Mark Lindsey, like Dennis Wilson of The Beach Boys, was every inch a sex symbol.

Mark was rather nice-looking, and seemed to me very self-centered when it came to women. Apparently, his libido was every bit as big as his ego, judging by what I observed while we were on the road. In spite of that, I found him to be a very nice young man, easy to travel with, and no problem at all for me. In fact, they were all pleasant to travel with. Mark just had a thing for girls, lots of them, and considering the opportunities, no one could blame him.

Before the tour was to start, I made a promotional swing through the cities we were going to play, just to check on any last minute details, and if necessary, to hype the ticket sales, which over-all were pretty good from the start. Paul Revere was at that time a "hot" group, which was the reason they were willing to pony up the expenses and pay for the promotion. They figured to make some very good money. I was covering two cities a day, which could be a little complicated when it came to making airplane connections, but that way, I didn't have to spend as much time out of the office. As I recall, the tour started in Austin, Texas.

When I arrived at the auditorium in time for rehearsal, the parking lot at the stage entrance was already crowded with young girls hoping for a look at or a wave from Mark Lindsey. I stood there awhile admiring the phenomenon of his attraction, when I noticed three young ladies standing off to one side, avoiding the crush. I asked why they weren't closer to the stage door like all the others. They said they weren't interested all that much, and they were just curious and wanted to see what was going on.

They were all sixteen years old, and I believe they were from San Marcos, or one of those nearby towns. Nothing exciting ever happened in San Marcos—or any of those nearby towns—and the chance to see Paul Revere and the Raiders was one they couldn't pass up, even though they had rather bad seats. I thought they were such nice girls that I offered to take them inside and let them watch the show from backstage, as long as they didn't get involved with any members of the band.

Sunny, Nancy, and Kathy turned out to be lovely young ladies who corresponded with me regularly and kept me advised of their personal plans over the next year. They had similar backgrounds in that each had father problems; either there was none at home at all, or he was abusive, but because of it, they became friends.

Nancy actually showed up in Los Angeles, calling me one Sunday morning at eight to tell me she was at the airport. I dressed, picked her up, and brought her home, where Phyllis and I found a place for her to rent in a private home. She was supposed to be in Austin, enrolling at the University of Texas, but she took her tuition money and bought an airplane ticket to Los Angeles instead.

She called every day to check in, as I asked, but eventually succumbed to someone's line about getting her in the movies. Unfortunately, she didn't believe the things I told her about Hollywood sleaze balls. She fell for some guy who was as phony as the proverbial $3 bill, and when she came down to earth, sadder, wiser, and no longer a virgin, I sent her back home to her family.

She was a very beautiful, but very naive young girl. Nancy did have some possibilities and I might have gotten her work as a model, but she met this guy and would only listen to him. She'd been a rodeo queen at sixteen, and a champion barrel rider. She was certainly pretty enough to have made it, but she, like so many girls looking for instant stardom, just couldn't wait. I lost track of her when she returned to school.

A DIFFERENT KIND OF EQUALITY

Our second show was in Baton Rouge, Louisiana, a beautiful little town about an hour west of New Orleans. While I was making the promotional tour, I stayed in New Orleans and then drove to Baton Rouge out along the bayous thick with mangrove trees, dripping with Spanish moss. I heard that the bayous were full of alligators, but even driving slowly, I failed to spot even one. Airplanes flying into New Orleans generally came in low over the bayous which gave you a quickie view. Mostly what you saw were the hundreds of trees that had been cut down, to prevent them from interfering with flight paths, I imagine.

It was in Baton Rouge that I had my first real taste of segregation. It was one thing to hear about restrooms for "colored only," but it was quite another to actually experience it. The date was at Louisiana State University (LSU), and it was there I first saw signs indicating white-only toilets and Black-only toilets. Naturally, I had to go into both of them, and it was true that the facilities were not the same. There was no such thing as "separate, but equal." The "colored" toilet was nowhere near as well-maintained. I mentioned my experience to members of the entertainment committee, but found that no one really gave a damn.

The people I dealt with would have denied there was any prejudice at the school, but certainly didn't seem to be ashamed of segregated toilets. They went to school with and freely associated with people of any color, but never seemed to understand that they hadn't yet gotten the message about equality. That was the way it was, the way of life, and anyone of them would have denied with great fervor that they harbored any racial or any other form of bigotry. After all, they liked me, and I was Jewish. The next stop was New Orleans. I don't remember much about the gig itself, which must mean there were no problems, but I do recall a party after the concert. My first trip to New Orleans was with Irving, but all I remember from *that* trip was finding a fast food restaurant late at night and eating great fried chicken. Irving and I stayed at a motel near the airport to facilitate our leaving, but I don't even recall why we were there.

WHY NOT EAT WELL ON SOMEONE ELSE'S DIME?

On my first "solo" trip to New Orleans to promote the date for Paul Revere and the Raiders, I asked the flight attendants for the name of the *best* restaurant in town, not necessarily the best-known, but where I could get absolutely the best food. As I was flying first class—I always went first class when it was on someone else's money—the stewardesses were very friendly. They were generally friendlier and more helpful to people in the expensive seats. A poll of the pilots and all the attendants came up with the name T. Pitari's.

T. Pitari's was well off the beaten path and nowhere near the tourist traps of Bourbon Street, Canal Street, or the Veaux Carre in the French Quarter. It was near Tulane University, but the cab driver knew exactly where it was. I was smart enough to make a reservation, and even with that had to wait about fifteen minutes. T. Pitari's was actually two restaurants in one.

On one side, it was a pretty standard Italian restaurant, and the other, featured the unusual. The menu showed items like buffalo, whale, and venison, but I went for the filet mignon and some sort of hot appetizer, which was a house specialty. The filet was about one and a half inches thick and tender enough to cut with my fork. From the crowd in both sections, obviously not the tourist trade, it was apparent I had made the right choice. The food confirmed it.

Of course, I spent the rest of the evening roaming about the Quarter like any tourist, going from one jazz joint to another, drinking a "Hurricane" in whichever bar claimed to be the most famous for it, and soaking up the atmosphere. It was as exciting as people claimed, but I discovered that walking the streets and haunting the shops on the side streets during the day was far more rewarding than Bourbon Street.

I found the tree-shaded streets and fantastic architecture of those outlying avenues were much more interesting—and a lot cheaper—than hitting the gin mills. A "Hurricane," by the way, was the most overrated drink in New Orleans, maybe in the whole world, unless getting a sugar diabetes attack was your idea of a good time.

Paul Revere's drummer, Joe Junior, was having his birthday, and Paul's Road Manager got the motel to give them some sort of recreation room for a party. I was assigned to pick up a girl because I had a car. The girl was very beautiful, but not very communicative on the drive back to the hotel. I did the best I could to involve her in conversation, but talking didn't seem to be her long suit. When we arrived at the party, I offered to get her something to drink or some cake, or whatever she wanted.

She said, "When are we going to fuck?"

I said, "This is Joe's birthday party and that's what we're here for. I, for one, intend to enjoy the party."

She said, "I came here because I was told I'd get to fuck one of the Raiders."

"Well," I said, "that lets me out because I don't qualify."

She said, "You're the producer, aren't you?" I answered that I was and she said, "Okay, then I'll fuck you." Don't get me wrong, I like beautiful women, but I'm not fond of stupid women—even if it meant getting laid. I still wanted to party for awhile, and so I walked over to one of the roadies and brought him over to her.

"John," I said, "this lady wants to get laid by a Raider. Why don't you oblige her?" He did, and I enjoyed the party. Not that I didn't have eyes for her; she *was* beautiful, but as I said, I have—and had—*some* standards, even on the road.

THE ONLY WAY TO FLY

My normal routine on the tour with Paul Revere and the Raiders was to work the date and then fly out the next morning to the next city, arriving well ahead of the band members, who were traveling on two buses. One was equipped with bunks in the back and seats up front for the band and crew. The second bus was for equipment, but also contained bunks for anyone who wanted peace and quiet.

I made one leg of the trip in the bus, and decided that first class air travel was much better.

The dates went without incident in Memphis, Tennessee and Jacksonville, Florida, except for one event in Memphis. I was backstage and ran into a girl who had driven there from Austin, Texas to see them again, but mostly because she wanted to get laid by Mark Lindsey. Somehow or other, she managed to get to Mark, and when I saw her again, she told me she had a date with him at two o'clock in the morning. Mark was making hourly dates and she was in line. I convinced her that she was being very foolish because even though she thought Mark was interested in her, she was just one of several dates he had that night. As far as I was concerned, he was interested only in a quick piece of ass because by the time she got to him, he had already set up three or four liaisons for earlier times. I assured her that there would be someone waiting to take her place when he was through and managed to talk her out of keeping the date. I did, however, introduce her to one of the roadies, whom I considered a nice young man, and they went out to dinner after the show.

The last stop, as I recall, was Macon, Georgia, a nice little city where the guys in the band did their best to get me in trouble. One thing we did not want to do in a strange town was get into trouble. The concert was a total sell out and the crowd was really on a high. Near the end of the show, one of the guys stood at the microphone and shouted, "Does everyone want to party tonight?"

The crowd roared back with its willingness, and whoever was at the microphone shouted back, "Meet us at the Holiday Inn, room 213 . . . Jack Lloyd's room."

Immediately after completing the details in the box office and turning over some money to Paul's Road Manager, I headed back to the hotel, only to find about 300 young people in the parking lot, all apparently ready to get into my room. There was one uniformed cop in the parking lot trying to keep some kind of order, and oddly enough doing very well. If nothing else, it was a well-behaved mob; dumb, but well-behaved.

I told the officer who I was and that I was going to hide myself in the hotel bar, which was in a separate structure at the front of the property, until everyone left, but that if he needed me for anything, he could find me there.

The lounge was already going full blast when I took a seat at the bar. They had a very good trio, the patrons were very friendly, and all were seemingly well on their way to intoxication. Within about ten minutes, some of the band members wandered in and we took a booth together. Mark was almost immediately recognized by some of the patrons, and soon they were sending drinks to us.

Mark asked me to find out if it was alright for him to play the organ when the trio took a break.

The organist said, "Sure, why not."

I had no idea he could play anything, but he really had talent. I turned to Joe Junior and said, "Why don't you go get a snare and a cymbal and set it up?"

When he came back with two roadies in tow, he had his entire drum set with him. The house trio played only organ, bass, and guitar. Someone picked up the guitar, another member of the band grabbed the bass, and they started to jam. They were having a good time and the bar patrons were being treated to some terrific improvisational jazz—not rock and roll. The regular trio sat down and didn't even try to go back on stage. Customers were dancing anywhere they could fit themselves between the tables and booths. The joint, as they say, "was really jumping."

At two o'clock in the morning when the bartender said, "Last call," there was a chorus of boos.

Mark said to me, "See if we can play a little longer."

The bar patrons were certainly up for it; they probably didn't have any place to go either and they were certainly enjoying the free show.

"Look," I said to the bartender, "what if we lock the doors to keep anyone from coming in and you stop selling booze? I'll tell the cop in the parking lot to hang around and play security. I'll even pay him a few bucks."

The very attractive waitress who assigned herself to our booth came over to me and said, "The cop ... he's my brother. He'll do whatever I ask, but only if I get to stay, too."

"Okay," I said to the bartender, "how's that?"

He shrugged his shoulders and said, "What the hell, let's do it."

A couple of guys in the band who were not jamming were coming on to our beautiful waitress, the sister of the cop. Sometime around three or four o'clock in the morning, the three of them left, but as it was just about time to wrap it up, I paid no particular attention.

The party finally broke up, and the roadies took the drum set back to the bus. I paid our bill and went upstairs to my room. The door was slightly ajar and I saw the waitress and the two members of the group on my bed. I could see she was not really happy with the idea and was doing her best to get up and out. Perhaps she changed her mind after they got to my room, but for whatever reason, she was certainly not happy when I got there. It never even occurred to me to ask how they got a key.

I AM ARMED

As far back as four or five years earlier, I had purchased a starter pistol. At one time, I was planning to be an AAU official for women's track and field, and I bought the gun and a very good stop watch. That was back in the days of hand-held timing, long before electronic timing was instituted. I started carrying it in my attaché case on those trips back before security checks were at airports, but of course, I had never used it for anything. The odds were pretty slim that I would run into a track meet, anyway.

When I couldn't get them to leave my room, I got the pistol out of my attaché case, put a tear gas pellet in it, and fired it towards them. It was just strong enough to get their attention.

The waitress thanked me for rescuing her, and the guys, not really unhappy because they weren't getting anywhere with her anyway, wanted to play with the pistol. I told them that if they left me alone and let me get some sleep, they could go have fun, but not in my room.

I loaded it with six tear gas pellets and turned them loose on the rest of the band, and I managed three hours sleep before having to hit the road back to Los Angeles.

CHAPTER NINE:
What I Did for "Love"—and Money

It would be a lie to say that I didn't like traveling. It did get in my blood. My father was a traveling salesman for more than thirty years until his death. He always wanted me to take his territory. After we moved to California in 1946, it stretched from Los Angeles to Lake Charles, Louisiana. Being a student at the University of Southern California, I had no intention of going on the road, and left it with, "I'll think about it after I graduate." I never did, not even for a minute.

Years later, when I had a taste of "the road" while traveling exclusively with and for Irving and then with The Beach Boys, there were times I *almost* wished I had taken him up on it. Traveling in the concert business, while involving work, was always fun. I am not against work. As they say, I could sit around and watch people do it all day. Work in the music business, at least from the production end, was mostly cerebral, although I loaded more than a few trucks, too.

Truthfully, selling souvenir books was a "no brainer." It didn't take a lot of smarts to count the number of books I started out with and subtract from that the number I had left to determine how many I had sold. When I was traveling without Irving, which turned out to be surprisingly often, including the entire DC-3 trip with The Beach Boys, it was my job to find sellers to help me; there was no way one person could cover all the doors and all the people. We generally sold books at intermission and on the walk-out, as well. We didn't want to miss anyone. Of course, I had some leeway when it came to giving books away. The act always wanted some, and I sometimes gave a few to pretty girls, newspaper people, or someone who really couldn't afford the $2, or someone from the auditorium management.

We had to account for every book, but as long as Irving or I didn't overdo the comps, there was never a problem. Irving and the act split the net profits. It was my job to make up the reconciliations and write the checks.

Some time around October 1967, Chad and Jeremy, the English act that was a hit on *The Beach Boys Summer Spectacular*, came to Irving about doing a small tour for them. We made inquiries around the country at radio stations, newspapers, and concert halls, and came to the conclusion that they wouldn't do very well as a headline act. We had a meeting and explained the results of our survey, but the boys decided they wanted to do it anyway if only to work out new material and music in front of live audiences. I thought it was a pretty expensive way to do it, but there was no talking them out of it.

We scheduled Texas concerts in Houston, Dallas, and Fort Worth, and some others including Panama City, Daytona Beach, and Orlando, in Florida. My memories of the trip mostly revolve around Dallas and Houston.

The southwest was an area Irving liked to travel, particularly at that time of the year because there were football games to attend on weekends. He had already purchased a pair of tickets on the fifty yard line to the Texas vs. Oklahoma University game at the Cotton Bowl, which was practically in downtown Dallas. The Texas/OU game was one of the big game rivalries in the country and he was looking forward eagerly to the trip, but fate once again intervened, and I went instead. I also got the tickets to the game. I was surprised Irving didn't want to sell them to me.

THERE'S MORE TO RUNNING A BOX OFFICE THAN I THOUGHT

Hilda Andrews, and her husband, Don, ran ticket sales in Houston and Dallas although they had no actual offices in Dallas, running the auditorium box office operations from their Houston base. She became my mentor in the intricacies of operating a box office. I had, to some extent, relied on the honesty of the people who ran the ticket offices, but Hilda thought I should learn all the tricks of the trade. Not how to cheat, but how to balance a box office quickly and how to keep from being cheated.

My first solo trip to Houston may have been with The Beach Boys. Hilda and Don decided to take me out for a few drinks after the concert. Houston was "dry" except in private clubs then, and they were either members or just very well-known at the Cork and Bottle, which was where they took me. We also took Hilda's assistant, Fay, with us. She didn't drink, but we fed her Shirley Temples for a couple of hours, telling her that there was alcohol in them, but very light. She got drunk. Don, who was a very heavy drinker, got himself pretty well polluted. Hilda and I got very friendly, to the point I had to question myself whether she was coming on to me or just trying to make her husband jealous.

Later that night, Hilda called me at the hotel and we spoke for perhaps an hour. I learned that she and Don were living together, but not having any sexual relations because Don, it turned out, was really homosexual. He managed to father four children with Hilda, but finally gave into his real feelings when he started a relationship with Fay's son, who was Hilda's hairdresser. The fact that she held the marriage together, really raised their kids alone, did all the work for their business, and still had time for other people endeared her to me, and obviously to others.

I think I have to say a couple more things about Hilda. She was about five-foot-eight and she always wore high heels. She was what you might call "willowy," although I always told her she was too thin. One day, she complained to me that she was "getting fat" and her weight had gone up to about 105 pounds. She was a beautiful woman, and she was literally loved by every promoter I ever knew. I always thought that Irving didn't want me to get too friendly with her because I suspect he had sexual feelings for her and didn't want me to get in the way in case something ever developed.

In her own way, she was very sexy. She would do just about anything for you and made you feel as though she was there just for you. Of course, I was like everyone else who knew her and fell in love with her.

Except that I always kidded her about her hair. She had lots of it and wore it in what I called a "Texas Fancy," sort of a "bee hive," which she had her hairdresser redo almost every day. I once asked her if her hair ever got messed up when she made love. She said, whoever it was had better not fool with her hair. I asked what happened when she went to sleep and she pointed out that one side was styled for her to lie on and that she did not move during the night.

Don was, when I met them, the ticket manager for the Houston Astros, so perhaps it was only natural that they should eventually open their own ticket office in Houston. There was no other real ticket broker there, and they helped scale the house for whatever group was brought in. It was also inevitable that Hilda created Quik-Tik, a company that not only printed tickets that couldn't be counterfeited, but scaled the house, which meant deciding how many tickets had to be sold at each price so we could get the average price we needed.

To sell their service, Hilda got in her Cadillac, which was all that she would drive, and set out around the country from one end to the other—east to west and south to north—making contracts with the various halls, theaters, arenas, and promoters in just about every major city. Since they could produce a set of tickets in a few days, promoters flocked to their service. Before Hilda, we were using Dillingham Ticket, which would take up to three weeks to print a set. Hilda's entire operation was computerized—she was the first to do it as far as I know—and there was little reason to use anyone else. She was a great salesperson and turned Quik-Tik into a big-time money-maker.

Basically, settling a box office amounted to counting the tickets that were left in each price range, which told us how many tickets were sold, once we deducted the comps. If we sold out, we already knew what should be in the till. It was when we didn't do well that counting tickets took time.

The Chad and Jeremy concerts did not do well in Houston, and there were lots of tickets to count. Today, there are machines that count the tickets and other machines to count the money, but then it was all done by hand. I realized that counting many tickets might take hours, but Hilda showed me how to count them by holding a stack to my ear and riffling through them. I found that counting by sound could be absolutely accurate. Money, on the other hand, was a little harder to count, especially if the bills were worn, but after a little practice I looked like W.C. Fields in *The Bank Dick*.

FAME IS FLEETING FOR THE FAMOUS

Standing in the Houston box office just after intermission, I was approached by three youngsters who wanted my autograph.

"Who do you think I am?" I asked.

They said they *knew* who I was, so there was no use in pretending. I had no idea who they thought I was. I was a little over six feet tall, wore my beard in a Van Dyke cut, and weighed in the neighborhood of 215 pounds. I couldn't think of any celebrity who looked like me.

"You're Pete Fountain," they said.

I denied it. They insisted. I said, "Pete Fountain comes up to here on me," pointing to an area about mid-way between my waist and shoulders. They were not to be dissuaded, so what else could I do? I signed their autograph books as Pete Fountain.

They wanted to know who Don Andrews was.

Don said, "Nobody," but they wouldn't believe him, so he ended up signing someone else's name.

ARE YOU READY FOR SOME FOOTBALL?

Before I left Los Angeles, I called ahead to Leighton Humphrey, Jr., a friend of Beach Boy Bruce Johnston, the one who flew him to Los Angeles when he jumped the airplane in Dallas after we left Tulsa. I called to let him know I'd be going to the game in Dallas and that I'd like to go with him. Irving told me Leighton would be hiring buses. He invited me to his aunt's home, from which the buses would leave for a "little pre-game lunch." Leighton said there would be a few friends over, and as long as I had an extra ticket, he would arrange a "date" for me for the game.

Leighton's aunt had a magnificent home in what seemed almost a private park, somewhere around the Mockingbird Lane area. She had the usual, neighborhood coterie of servants who were busy serving when I got there.

His aunt took me around to meet people, and then led me to a table with about $10,000 worth of food spread out.

"Ahm truly sorry for this misahable spray-ed," she said in her deep Texas drawl, "Leighton didn't give me much tahm to put anahthang togetha." I accepted her apology. Then she apologized for not having enough serving people; "It's so hahd to get good hep these dayahs. I jus don't know wheah all the good dahkies have gone."

I doubt that she was prejudiced when it came to the color of their skin. She would certainly have denied it, but then, she probably would have denied there was anything wrong with having slaves. After all, didn't their masters treat them well? At least that's what I think she might have said. One of the privileges of being rich, I suppose. Not an excuse for it, but just a fact of Texas life.

If there wasn't quite enough food to feed the entire US 5th Army, there was enough booze to give the entire population of Dallas a serious high and a major hangover. Dallas, on the weekend of the Texas/OU game, was total insanity. Old grads from both schools generally came for the entire week and partied until some time after the game.

It didn't seem to matter which team the old grads were rooting for; they all seemed hell-bent-for-leather to do their best to destroy the city, or at the very least, their hotel rooms. The downtown hotel where I stayed was raining furniture from the upper stories the night before the game, and I approached the door cautiously, my eyes turned skyward. According to the morning paper, the police incarcerated more than 900 people by putting them in the clink overnight and then letting them go in time for the game.

Leighton announced that it was time to go. I, my date, and about thirty other revelers piled into one of the two buses waiting at curbside. I never could have made it in my own car. Not only would I never have found my way into the parking lot, but it took a maniacal bus driver to intimidate enough drunk drivers to force his way inside. Then, too, there was a special section close to the stands for buses. Each of our buses came equipped with a bar and bartender so no one would have to stop drinking before they got to the game. Our bus was also equipped with two television sets and some people never made it into the stadium.

The young lady who was my "date" for the game and I took very tall glasses of Jack Daniels and water with us, so we wouldn't run dry for at least the first quarter of the game. For some idiotic reason, I felt obligated to drink on a par with my host and his guests.

Our drinks lasted into the second quarter, and at half-time we found our way back to the bus for refills. Even more astoundingly, we made it back to our seats in time for the rest of the game. I have no idea who won, but the Texas people didn't seem miserable afterwards, so maybe they did. On the other hand, maybe they were all just drunk and it really didn't matter who won after all.

BACK TO WORK

I had a concert that night, and as the hour grew later, we still weren't moving very quickly in the exiting traffic. I began to worry a little about getting to the hall in time to start the show. Leighton assured me that I had plenty of time, and I foolishly took his word for it, not that I could have done anything about it. No matter what, I still had to get back to my car.

By the time we got to Leighton's aunt's home I was really pressed for time. My "date" had a real date for the evening, and so I wasn't expected to take her to the concert, dinner, or anything like that, which was just as well.

Considering the fact that I had only a vague idea how to get to the auditorium, I still managed to get to there about ten minutes before curtain. Chad and Jeremy were more than a bit upset that I hadn't been there in the afternoon for rehearsal until I reminded them that they knew I going to the game.

The concert got started on time, finished on time, and I got the box office settled on time, and they actually made a little money on the date, which pleased them.

Hilda had run the box office from her home in Houston and was in town to handle sales and settlement at the auditorium that night. She brought her friend/hairdresser/box office assistant, Fay, with her, but I didn't want to take both of them to dinner after the show. Besides, I already had plans for the evening.

I explained to her that I was going to Fort Worth to visit friends following the show and didn't expect to get back to the hotel until around two o'clock in the morning, which was the truth. I suggested that there was no sense in her hanging around, and that if she didn't already have a place to stay, she might be able to get a room at the motel where I was staying. Or, if she decided to go back home, I would see her in Houston.

When I got back to my room in Dallas, Hilda, Fay, and another of Hilda's friends, Betty (or Betsy) Sue was there, waiting in my room. Hilda told the girl at the desk she was my wife and they gave her the key. It seemed that all three of them were planning to stay the night with me.

I had always wanted to have a sexual encounter with two or three women at the same time, but Hilda was married to a guy I knew, Fay wasn't very attractive, and Betty/Betsy Sue didn't say three words to me. Not that conversation was a prerequisite for sex. As some sage once said, "Some of the best time I have ever had, hardly a word was spoken."

Besides, I didn't think a "quartet" was in the works and I doubted that under any circumstances I would have been up to it. Fortunately, the room had a couch and the three ladies got to sleep together in the bed, although Hilda did offer to let me sleep with her and Fay, or maybe her and Betty/Betsy.

Some time later, on another trip to Dallas or Houston, I heard from Betty/Betsy Sue. She told me she had wanted to get together with me that night, but couldn't figure a way to talk to me with Hilda and Fay there. She got up in the middle of the night and walked to the toilet without her clothes on, hoping to get my attention. She certainly did that. I do recall that she was very pretty and had a nice body. Some time later, Hilda told me that she was twenty-eight years old and had five ex-husbands already.

The rest of the tour was uneventful. Chad and Jeremy did lose money, but as Irving made his usual 10 percent deal, and as Chad and Jeremy covered my expenses, Irving made out like a bandit.

CHAPTER TEN:
A Family Reunion
Begins—Almost

Irving Granz and Norman, who was his brother and a jazz impresario, hadn't gotten along with one another for several years. The best that could be said of them was that Norman did his best to ignore Irving. Norman's US office was just down the hall from mine, run by Mary Jane Outwater, who had been with Norman for years. She actually ran the day-to-day operations of Salle Productions ("Salle" is "Ella's" spelled backwards, for Ella Fitzgerald), but she was also Norman's assistant in his other business activities. He kept an office there to use whenever he flew in from Europe—and, I guess, to store his excess Picassos. Norman was, as I understood it, one of the most important collector's of Picasso's works and a frequent visitor to his home in Spain.

Norman and Irving's mother had been ill for some time, and with the worsening of her condition, Norman was spending more time in Los Angeles. He was supposedly limited to thirty days a year because he had moved a few years earlier to Europe to escape US taxes. Because of her illness, he and Irving were forced to see one another often.

Practically on her death bed, Mrs. Granz extracted a promise from both brothers that they would get back together and be friends. Norman had been planning a *Jazz at the Philharmonic* retrospective tour with Ella Fitzgerald, Oscar Peterson, and some of the great jazz names who worked for him over the years, sort of a "JATP Revisited."

As an olive branch, Norman asked Irving to set up the cities and dates, with Norman's approval of course, and to produce a souvenir book. We both put all our efforts into making that tour a huge success because it would have been very prestigious for Irving and also very rewarding for him financially.

Norman was back in Europe during the time we were arranging venues and making radio and newspaper deals, returning only after we had almost completed setting up the tour. Everything pointed to a hugely successful venture.

The design and layout for the souvenir book was pretty much finished, thanks to Gordon Green, the best "book artist" in the business. I think a "blue line" had already been completed, or maybe a dummy rough had been put together to show Norman when he returned.

Norman hated the book. Personally, I think it was an excellent book, but whatever Norman didn't like about it brought back all the old animosities between them. Norman took over the book, saying that Irving should just forget it, and that he would do it over and do it right. In the end, the book was almost exactly as Gordon Green had designed it, but with only a few minor changes. It seemed to me that for some reason, Norman just wouldn't accept the fact that Irving had some talent for the business.

Irving was already committed to another short tour with some act when Norman showed up. I was going to go along to sell books, so we had to leave Los Angeles with everything very much up in the air and Irving a nervous wreck.

We landed in, I think, St. Louis, and Irving stopped at a pay telephone in the airport to check his messages. There was a call from Norman. Irving called him immediately, and for the next twenty or so minutes they screamed at one another. Of course, I could only hear Irving's end of the "conversation," but I could surmise Norman's. It was not at all pleasant.

Irving hung up the telephone and said, "I'm going to grab the next airplane back to Los Angeles. I'll catch up with you somewhere." He stayed in the airport and I went into town. I did the date and went on to wherever the second date was scheduled when Irving joined me.

"You've got to go back today," he said, and "talk to my brother. He won't talk to me."

Irving had already invested $25,000 of his own money in the

JATP tour, and Norman essentially told him to go screw himself. Irving could hardly afford to lose that much money even though he did very well on his own in the concert and book business. He certainly couldn't afford to eat that kind of loss. Norman apparently had no intention of repaying Irving's investment, but he seemed willing to talk to me even though he wouldn't consider talking to Irving. I was supposed to go back and talk to Norman and convince him to give Irving back his money. It was actually the first time I ever said more than a dozen words to Norman.

I GET TO KNOW THE MONSTER

We met in Norman's office, which wasn't much of an office. It was located at the end of the hall and consisted of an outer "secretarial" office, and his small office was behind that. What did impress me was the number of Picasso originals leaning against the wall.

I had all of Irving's record books with me, as well as copies of all the bills and as many canceled checks as I could gather. I was fully prepared to take on the ogre. Never having had a real conversation with Norman, I had no idea what to expect, but from Irving's description, I imagined he would be, at the very least, breathing fire and reeking of sulfur and brimstone.

Actually, Norman and I got on very well. He had no arguments with me; he was very pleasant and easy to talk to except when Irving's name came up. After ten or fifteen minutes of small talk, apparently to give Norman a chance to size me up, he got serious and gave me his entire attention. Putting it mildly, he wasn't happy with his brother. He had the attitude, I thought, that Irving would never be smart enough to be a successful concert producer, even though Irving already had a number of major successes to his credit.

Although I think maybe Norman really wanted to screw Irving out of the money to teach him some kind of lesson, after a few days of negotiating, he relented and wrote a check for the entire $25,000, which I put in the bank immediately, before Norman had a chance to change his mind. Norman might have been the toughest man in the world to deal with (other than promoter Bill Graham), but I decided that once he made up his mind to do something, he would do it. However, he also decided that Irving was out as far as the tour was concerned.

My knowledge of Norman was pretty much limited to his publicity and what Irving and some friends had to say about him. When he moved to Europe and was told that he could spend only thirty days a year in the United States, Norman decided the government couldn't possibly consider the time he was in the air, and that as he didn't usually work on weekends, they couldn't count that against him. They also couldn't count the hours when he was asleep, and they couldn't count the hours when he was merely socializing or visiting his mother; they were only entitled, he reasoned, to count the actual hours he was working.

The only other story I know about Norman, which says a lot about the man, was related to me by Mo Ostin, Norman's comptroller at Verve, Norgran, and Clef and whatever other record labels Norman operated. Anyway, the story Mo told related to a time when The Bell Telephone Company wanted to feature Ella Fitzgerald on *The Bell Telephone Hour*.

Norman agreed as long as the deal included Ella's trio, which included her husband (or ex-husband perhaps, by then), Ray Brown, and at least one white musician. When the producers at the television show saw that it was a "mixed" group, they balked.

The story, as Norman related it to Mo, was that the telephone company didn't want to show Blacks and Whites together because "we have lots of customers in the south who won't like it." Norman wanted Ella on the show because of the prestige, but wouldn't allow anyone else to play for her. They compromised and decided that the trio could play, but only behind a scrim, which was a sort of filmy, translucent material that would mask the skin color of the group. Ella performed as required, but the next day, Norman took full-page ads in the *Los Angeles Times* and the *New York Times* relating the entire story. There may have been other papers as well, but I only know of the two. I think that speaks volumes as to the character of the man.

STAGING A CONCERT IS NOT
ALL FUN AND GAMES

Incidentally, as I've said, Irving did not produce *all* the concerts for The Beach Boys. Their booking agency sold most of them, but whenever there were open dates, they offered them to Irving. He might do only two or three fill-in shows on any given tour. When those openings occurred, we got busy trying to find locations that fit their travel schedule and which made sense financially. Because of that, we booked The Beach Boys in places like Waterloo, Iowa, where their "dressing room" was the stables in which horses had been stored for the rodeo only a day or two before. Irving made enough money from his Beach Boy dates and from souvenir book sales to finance his other concerts.

He booked rock guitarist Jimi Hendrix in Boston, and The Rolling Stones somewhere up north, perhaps Oregon. According to Irving, both gigs lost money. His reconciliations were always on scraps of paper, and I had to make sense of them for the accountant. In Boston, Irving had to hire so many extra police that the costs exceeded the gross, or so he said. Irving may have booked The Rolling Stones a little too early in their career. It happened to me a few years later when I booked and produced a show with Mike Zugsmith, whose wife had worked for me when I was in the publishing business. We headlined Fleetwood Mac, unfortunately about three months before they hit it big. If someone hadn't broken into the box office and stolen a bunch of tickets, we would have lost our ass. The box office had to make good on them.

Irving had been doing pretty well financially, and on his way home from some tour in the east, he stopped in Las Vegas where he dropped at least $8,000 at the tables. I say "at least," because that was the amount of the check I had to write to cover his markers. He really couldn't afford to lose that much money, which is why I was very surprised when he gave me a Christmas bonus of $2,000. I think it was a combination of guilty conscience and the influence of his accountant, who also tried to convince Irving that he ought to give me a raise. Otherwise, he would have ended up giving it to Uncle Sam. Irving decided against it.

That led to a conversation about more money for me and Irving's comment that if I was ever offered more money by anyone, I should take it. I must also add that I was then making about $200 a week, which was a $50 raise from the previous year. That remark led me to consider a "feeler" that came my way at the end of 1967.

CHAPTER ELEVEN:
Temptation Rears Its Financial Head

Sometime around September or October 1967, Dick Duryea, The Beach Boys Road Manager, called me at Irving's office. He asked whether or not Irving was around because he didn't want him to overhear my end of the conversation. When I assured him that Irving was out, Dick said that The Beach Boys were considering dropping Irving as their occasional producer. He explained that Nick Grillo, their Business Manager, thought they should book and produce their own open dates and save the 10 percent they were paying Irving.

"So, why are you telling me this?" I asked.

"I just wanted to know if you thought we could do it."

I said, "Look, Irving does a good job for you, and besides, he goes along on dates that aren't his, just to help out, so in essence you get another body practically for free on some dates."

"Yeah, we know all that, but Nick has got the guys convinced they don't need Irving, so it's probably going to happen anyway. I just wanted your opinion."

"Well," I said, "if you're not too stupid, and I don't think you are, you'll only make mistakes once and after that you'll get along fine."

"And if we have troubles, we can always go back with Irving."

"I'm sure he'll be happy to take them back."

"Don't say anything yet, because it's not completely settled."

Dick and Irving got along very well on the road, and I was sure Dick would try to dissuade them. I didn't know Nick all that well, but I did know he once worked for an accounting firm that took care of The Beach Boys books and taxes before he talked them into hiring him as their full-time Business Manager, and to taking offices in the 9000 Sunset Boulevard building.

They also tried to start their own record company, Brother Records, while they were at the 9000 building, but I gather it was pretty much a disaster. Reams of material concerning that effort have been written in books and articles about The Beach Boys, so there is no sense in my recounting the record company fiasco here.

In January or February 1967, Nick called Irving to inform him that The Beach Boys intended to try and produce an entire tour themselves. Irving was a little upset, but we were so busy doing other dates with other acts that he didn't seem overly concerned—then.

As I had more than enough work to do, writing publicity releases, writing and creating display ads, running the office, and occasionally going on the road to handle book sales, it didn't make much difference to me one way or the other. On top of it, Irving was having problems with his wife, and I spent a large part of my time playing the role of his amateur psychologist.

In late February or March, Dick called to tell me about the *Million Dollar Tour* he had mapped out covering a number of southern and southeastern cities plus a few more dates in Texas. I think that a few of the dates were to be sold to independent promoters, but most would be paid for by The Beach Boys. It was a risky investment because they were not at that time nearly as popular as they had been. It had nothing to do with their talent, but it did have something to do with the fact that they had not produced any "hits" in some time and were somewhat out of the limelight. Consequently, they did not have a lot of cash reserves. Historically, they had done well in that part of the country and they expected to pick up a lot of money.

Dick also asked whether I would consider coming over to work with him at American Productions, The Beach Boys corporate designation for concert touring.

He threw out a tentative dollar amount, more than Irving was paying me. I said I would certainly *consider* any offer, but that I still owed some loyalty to Irving both as an employer and as a friend. He understood and made it clear that he was just asking to see if I might be interested in case it ever came up.

A few days later, the opportunity came up to tell Irving that I had received a tentative offer of better money. I didn't tell him where it came from because I knew what his reaction would have been, and besides it was only tentative.

He said, "If you get a better offer, you should go." I said that I felt an obligation to him, but that I could use a little more money.

Irving's response was that he couldn't afford to pay me any more. Considering what I knew of his income and expenses, losses in Las Vegas, and other extravagances, I was fully aware that he could have come up with much more than the $200 a week I was getting. What's more, his accountant kept telling him that he had too much money in his corporate account and that he ought to give me a raise. If he didn't do something like that, the accountant told me, he'd end up giving it to the government. Either give me a raise or buy me a car was his suggestion. Irving did go as far as telling me to go look for a car, but then kept putting it off, and in the end, he just passed on the raise and the car. He did make some sort of an attempt to console me by buying me an expensive sport coat at Dick Carroll's haberdashery in Beverly Hills. I presume it was expensive because *everything* was expensive at Dick Carroll's.

A DECISION GETS IMPERATIVE

April 1968 came and The Beach Boys started out on their big tour. Opening night was in Memphis, Tennessee. They had a good-sized audience, possibly even a sold-out house. They were just getting ready to go on stage when the National Guard entered the hall, asked them to leave the premises, and ordered the audience to go home. The date was April 4, and Martin Luther King, Jr. had just been shot to death.

Because of the volatile situation in the south, The Beach Boys would have to cancel or reschedule most of their dates. *The Million Dollar Tour* was beginning to look like a million dollar bust. Dick told me they were facing a loss in excess of $100,000 unless they could somehow reschedule the dates without adding too much to their budget.

On April 5, I got a call from Nick Grillo. He said, "You know what Dick was talking to you about?"

I said, "Yes, of course." Up to that moment, I had no idea where the tour was starting other than "the south," and I had no idea of the impact that King's murder had on their plans.

"Would you consider coming over here to work now?"

"What do you mean, 'now'?"

"Right away, today."

I told him there was no way I would leave Irving without notice, and that I would have to discuss it with him first. I owed him that much. Then I asked him the more important question, "How much?"

Nick offered me $300 a week plus expenses, and the promise of a contract with built-in escalations.

I went to Irving and told him what I had been offered, but that it was contingent on my leaving immediately—without any notice. His answer made my choice easy.

"I told you if you ever got a better offer to take it."

Nick had asked me not to tell Irving I was going with them, at least not immediately. He had his reasons, and I agreed, but I'm not sure why, and it was probably wrong not to tell him.

If you recall, I said that Irving was not particularly upset when Nick told him that they were not going to use his services. I presume that Nick said something like, "We'll use you again later," although I have no way of knowing what actually occurred during their conversation. What I do know is that Irving eventually accused me of "stealing" The Beach Boys from him, which of course was ridiculous. They left him about six months before they ever called me.

I DO HAVE THE EXPERTISE

The plan was for me to come to The Beach Boys new offices on Ivar Street in Hollywood and pick up an airplane ticket to Jacksonville, Florida, where the entire troupe had moved while they decided what to do. My immediate job would be to reschedule the entire tour as quickly as possible, and to get them back on the road.

I flew into Jacksonville the next day and met with Dick Duryea for several hours. They were fortunate in that some of the dates in Texas would not be affected, and as plans already included a more or less circular route, we still would be able to end the tour in Miami Beach, Florida, where they had always been successful.

After four or five days on the telephones, Dick and I managed to agree on a tour that would work. We combined some of the previously set dates in Texas with a few new locations, in some cases playing two cities a day, like Corpus Christi and Brownsville, as day and night affairs. Contrary to comments in a 1978 book by David Leaf about The Beach Boys, the tour was not canceled; it was only re-routed. Leaf also referred to Nick Grillo as an attorney, which was also untrue. He was not even, at that time certainly, a *certified* public accountant.

I DIGRESS FOR A MOMENT

That brings up a point I would like to make about Irving's way of doing things, which I adopted. He never did a concert that didn't involve reserved seating, a practice I continued throughout my "career" in the music business. Having reserved seats prevented any riots, kept people from getting hurt, and made for a better concert experience for everyone.

"Open" or "Festival" seating, in my opinion, was the worst thing that ever happened to the indoor concert business. The promoters who allowed rushing the stage thought it was a wonderful idea because there was so much enthusiasm, but I will always believe that allowing the audience to rush the stage was responsible for most of the physical problems that began to beset the concert business, both in damage to halls and injuries—even deaths—to the audience. I hated the idea then, and still do.

If you will allow me to digress a little longer, I will relate an experience at the San Francisco Cow Palace at *The Beach Boys Summer Spectacular* in 1966.

We knew, because of the large number of "San Francisco" groups on the show, and because San Francisco promoter Bill Graham had open seating at his Fillmore West shows, we would need extra police to control the crowd. We had been warned that the crowd would expect to go to the stage once the concert started. The Cow Palace held more than 15,000 people, and we were sold out. As I said, we preferred to keep the audience in their seats during the performance, letting small groups at a time approach the stage to take photographs. We also tried to keep them sitting so that everyone would be able to see the show.

We used ushers to keep everyone seated and deployed police in front of regular police sawhorse barricades that were set about five feet in front of the stage, because we had entered the era of kids leaping on stage during the performance. Even with the barricades, we intercepted more than a few trying to get to or *at* the performers.

I stationed myself behind the barricades to direct police and our other security to trouble spots—and because I felt a lot safer behind them than in front of them. Several times, I vaulted the sawhorses to restrain raucous Bay Area fanatics. At one point, after having jumped the barricades perhaps ten times, I vaulted over once more and my hamstring muscles locked. I couldn't move. I was stuck in front of on-rushing Grace Slick fans. For a split second, I could see myself being trampled to death, before a cop could get to me. Fortunately, one *did* get there just ahead of a bunch youngster hell-bent for the stage.

Something like that happened to me again in Phoenix, Arizona, where I had gone to supervise the sale of souvenir books for Sly and The Family Stone at the Convention Center. Sly attracted real crazies and druggies, and because there was unreserved seating, the crowd began gathering at least two hours early.

It was obvious the audience was getting antsy and wanted in. Civilian security people came to block the glass doors and to keep the crowd from breaking through. Not too long before that event, someone had been killed in Cincinnati when they surged through the doors and trampled a young girl, which was one of the big problems with festival or unreserved seating.

I found myself standing with the security people behind a row of about four doors, which were beginning to bow inward. I was helping security people, who were trying hard to hold the doors shut from the increasingly surly crowd.

Suddenly, I realized what I was doing, turned to the guard at my side, and said, "I don't know what the fuck I'm doing here; this isn't my show." I got out of the way just before the doors were smashed open and several thousand people began the mad dash for the front of the auditorium.

CHAPTER TWELVE:
Making It All Work

In Florida, where Dick Duryea and I finished assembling the rebuilt tour, Dick had hired an "opening act" to travel with them, a hot young group called Buffalo Springfield with Neil Young, Steven Stills, Richie Furay, Jim Messina, and drummer Dewey Martin. They were idled along with The Beach Boys in Florida, spending most of their time at the pool soaking up the sun.

Dewey Martin was the group's ladies man. He was married to a beautiful girl, who I think was a former Miss Something-or-other. He carried several 8x10 glossies of her in provocative poses—bikinis and that sort of thing—with him everywhere. He told me he used them to get girls up to his room with a line something like, "What makes you think I want you to go to bed with me? I'm married to the most gorgeous girl you ever saw. If you come up to my room, I'll show you her pictures."

It was reminiscent of an old gag line that goes: "One of the things I like about southern girls with their slow drawl is that when you ask them for sex, by the time they get around to saying 'no', it's too late."

Neil Young was a very quiet, almost shy young man. I found myself in his room from time to time while he played his most recent composition for my edification and opinion. I have no idea why he thought *my* opinion meant anything, but then maybe he was just being polite to an older man.

When it got too late in the day for Dick and me to work the telephones, and while we were hard at work drinking, loafing around, or in the hotel pool, Neil went off by himself to write.

When I finally rejoined the tour and saw him on stage for the first time, I offered him a little suggestion. I said, "Neil, you really have to turn around and face the audience when you play. No one is interested in your worn out, baggy jeans. Besides, your ass doesn't fill them up."

I remember The Buffalo Springfield as basically nice young men with outstanding talent. Stephen Stills supposedly had a little ego problem, but he never caused any problems for me nor the tour. In fact, one night he bought me dinner at Wolfie's or maybe Pumpernick's, on Collins Avenue. The other members of the band thought I should consider myself honored.

I believe it was in Miami Beach that Steve got in some trouble, although it could have been an earlier stop. I was told that he picked up a woman somewhere, took her to his room, and did what one does when one picks up a woman and takes her to his room.

Apparently, she asked for money when it was all over, and because it was all over, Stephen said, "no way," or something akin to that. I suppose it could have been a bit earthier, but then again, I wasn't there. She went to the cops and complained that she had been raped. I suppose she thought that not getting paid was the equivalent of getting raped.

As the story was related to me, the police picked him up, and when the group was preparing to leave for the next date, Stephen was nowhere to be found. They checked all the local hospitals and police stations where they finally found him. Fortunately, one of the officers knew the woman in question and was aware she had done this sort of thing before, so they let him go.

THE NEWEST HOLLYWOOD GURU

Before I joined them, The Beach Boys were already deeply involved with the Maharishi Mahesh Yogi and Transcendental Meditation. They met the Maharishi in Paris not too long after The Beatles started their public sponsorship of the guru and decided to get initiated as a group. Mike Love was so taken with the Maharishi, he promised that The Beach Boys would set up a lecture tour of American colleges for him.

The plan was for The Beach Boys to open the "show" with a full set, and then the Maharishi would come out after intermission and lecture. The Maharishi wanted to contact young men and women of college age, feeling that if they used TM they would increase their capacity to learn and retain information. I asked him later how he felt that would work. He likened the use of TM to drawing on a bowstring. For example, if you started with a hundred-pound pull, you might be able to pull it back only a few inches, but the more you pulled, the farther you would be able to pull it. As we use only a small portion of the brain, TM, he insisted, would enable you to use more and more by continued and repeated use. *Why not?* I wondered.

He pushed The Beach Boys to do it for him. I gathered that The Beatles weren't interested. I didn't think much of the idea, but they were my employers and I did what I was asked. It sounded pretty dull to me, but I have to admit it didn't turn out that way. The Maharishi was a very commanding presence, but even more compelling for me was that he was a very nice, friendly man.

Mike Love, Alan Jardine, and Carl Wilson were very much involved with TM and were already practicing it when I joined them. Bruce Johnston had been initiated and seemed involved to a lesser degree. Dennis went through the motions only to please his brother and cousin, but Dennis was not the type to make commitments to much of anything. Mike was far and away the most serious disciple of the Maharishi.

As soon as Dick and I completed rescheduling the tour, Mike sent me to New York to meet with an agent they hired some months earlier to line up colleges for the Maharishi dates. Bookings had not been going well, if at all, and my job was to put together a tour in under two weeks.

I checked in at the Hilton in mid-town Manhattan and asked for a room as high above the street as I could get. I wanted to be as far away from the street and lobby noise as possible. They found a room for me on the 45th floor. Secure in the knowledge that I would get a good night's rest before plunging into what I knew was going to be a tough sell, I crawled into bed early.

At six-thirty the next morning, I was awakened by the sound of jack hammers, yelling workmen, and the clanging of steel beams. I thought I was somehow transported to a lower floor. There was no choice but to get up because the noise level made further sleep impossible. I pulled back the drapes and was greeted with the sight of a building under construction or perhaps demolition one floor below mine.

After about ten days of pretty concerted effort, working with one of the secretaries, who also took me around to some of the small, interesting, and out-of-the-way restaurants, we managed to work out deals with eight or nine private, east coast promoters.

Although it was supposed to be a "college" tour, there was no time to do it that way. Colleges had long since booked their own dates for the coming season, so I decided on an alternate plan.

We contacted promoters who could guarantee a performance either at or in conjunction with a school. The school would get a piece of the gate for the use of their name and facilities, if that could be worked out. As The Beach Boys were not charging for their performance—other than expenses—the Maharishi would get the bulk of the proceeds, less the promoter's profits and the school's cut. The money was earmarked to help build the future Maharishi International University.

REJOINING MY EMPLOYERS

I satisfied myself that everything was under control, that we had made sufficient contacts to assure the beginnings of a tour, and that the girl I was working with could continue contacting bookers. I extracted a promise from the agent and his staff that they would arrange additional dates on the west coast and hit the road to meet the group in Texas before the tour headed back to Florida, where we would end at the Convention Center in Miami Beach.

By playing two shows a night or a day/night concert, and using limousines to send The Buffalo Springfield ahead to the next city as they finished their stint, the tour started making some money, or at least making up some of the loss. I remember Dallas as being a very big date. We were there a few days ahead of time because we hadn't been able to fill every night on our makeshift rerouted tour. We used the extra time to garner some extra publicity with radio and newspaper interviews.

Dick Duryea and I arranged a dinner meeting at our hotel with a reporter from the *Dallas Morning News*. The reporter turned out to be a much more than attractive young woman towards whom Dick took an immediate turn. It was obvious to me that the turn was mutual. I certainly was not going to interfere with any plans they might make, but they kindly insisted I stay with them for dinner, which I did while they played footsie.

Dennis Wilson was in the same dining room, eating and drinking with his cousin, Steve Korthoff, our equipment manager, and Jon Parks. Jon was more-or-less the assistant sound man and actually Dennis' friend, who was on payroll to help Dennis with his drag racing hobby and anything else he needed done. I don't know what they ate, but I recognized the Dom Perignon bottles that kept arriving at their table, as Dennis, who rarely exhibited good taste in anything, was at least ordering the right bubbly.

I stayed with Marge and Dick until we finished dinner, and then I excused myself to join Dennis and his guests.

When the occasion called for it, Dennis could be extremely persuasive with the ladies. He was already in full flirt with the strikingly beautiful waitress serving his table, and her resistance to his charms was rapidly evaporating.

At first, she declined his offer to join him after work, but finally gave him her telephone number to call after she finished her shift. She was taking a big chance because the hotel had rules against employees fraternizing with guests, especially in their hotel rooms.

Dennis ordered three more bottles of Dom Perignon, which he wanted to drink in my room, but I knew what would happen if we went there, and I had plans for a quiet evening. Steve Korthoff volunteered his room, so we adjourned there to finish the wine and wait until Dennis made his call.

The four of us repaired to Steve's room with the three bottles of Dom Perignon, one of which Dennis wanted to keep for the waitress he fully expected would join him. I really didn't want him to get involved, first because if she got caught coming into the hotel and going into an elevator, she was sure to get fired, and second because Dennis was in a crazy mood from all the wine.

About an hour after we left the dining room, maybe less, Dennis made his call. She answered immediately; it was obvious she had been waiting. Dennis held the telephone away from his ear so that we could hear her say that she was very flattered, but she was having second thoughts. Dennis was never one to quit when he was after a woman. He told her that if she got fired, he'd get her another job, which of course he couldn't, but she apparently believed him or was at least willing to take the chance.

We tried talking her out of it by yelling at the telephone over Dennis. We were sort of "kidding on the square" because we really didn't think it was a good idea. Dennis didn't think it was funny, and when Dennis didn't think something was funny, there was no telling what he might do. We kept at it until he took the telephone under the blankets.

As soon as the young lady gave in, Dennis crawled out from under the covers, no longer in a good mood. He was, in fact, pissed. Dennis was often given to violent mood swings for no reason at all, but then he had a reason. He expressed his displeasure by ripping the telephone out of the wall and throwing the bed, mattress and all, against the window. Dennis was very strong. I thought he was over-reacting and told him so in no uncertain terms.

"Not only am I upset at your reaction," I said, "you are going to give your room to Steve and you're going to use this room." He said he would rent another room, and I told him he would not, and he calmed down. "Just put everything back or fuck her in the tub," I said. I guess he put the room back together enough because they stayed there. Sometime that night, he decorated the bathtub, which I learned about when I went to settle the bill.

"I painted a picture," he said.

"Where?" I asked.

"In the tub. I thought it needed brightening up. It's red."

"What's red?"

"The picture. It's a nude. I used her nail polish. Maybe you'd better tell the manager."

I didn't bother to check out the quality of his art. Art to Dennis was most likely stick figures, anyway, but I did call the hotel manager, told him what happened, and asked him to send a bill for repairs to our office.

IT'S NOT EASY WITHOUT THE GREEN

Traveling provided another little problem. Nick Grillo, the Business Manager, wouldn't give me or Dick a company credit card. Before I came with American Productions, Nick had convinced Dick to put the bills, sometimes more than a couple thousand dollars, on his own card, and then Nick would reimburse him at the end of a tour from the money they collected along the way. Once I actually settled into the routine of my job, I did the same thing. It turned out to be a serious mistake for both of us because there came a time when Nick kept holding back on our money. By the time we got paid, our credit cards had been canceled.

THE REST OF THE TOUR/IRVING'S REVENGE

As we worked our way towards Miami Beach, I kept in contact with Tom Jefferson, a promotion man Irving used over the years and whom we hired to ramrod that date. Tom told me that Irving had managed somehow to book a concert in the same building the night before ours, something no reputable auditorium manager or promoter would ever do. It was common courtesy to give the first booking some protection, usually at least one week before and after.

Tom suspected, but couldn't prove, that Irving offered the manager a lot of money to give him the date. I don't recall the act, but it was a major name, and we were, to say the least, very upset. A call to the manager got me lots of double talk, but no satisfaction. Because of Irving's show, our ticket sales had slowed to a crawl. It looked as though Irving would extract some measure of revenge for our defection.

I left the tour and flew ahead to meet with Tom Jefferson, hoping we could think of some way to salvage that very important date. Even though he was an old friend of Irving's, Tom was very upset at what he had done and willing to help us in any way. He booked interviews for me with the papers and on radio, and we increased our advertising budget.

The night of our performance finally arrived, and Dick and I were in the box office wondering whether or not there were enough people left in town with any money to get us into the black. Dick spotted Irving outside, watching the walk-up sale. He was certain he killed our show because his was reasonably successful.

About an hour before show time, people began lining up at the box office. The lines grew longer and longer, and soon it became obvious we would have to delay the show to accommodate everyone who wanted tickets. Irving disappeared into the night. Before we started the show, we were sold out or damn close to it, and presumably Irving went home with his tail between his legs.

Photo Gallery

First of three pictures of the "new" Beach Boys image. One of the first projects I had done when I took over as head of American Productions.

**Backstage at the Ed Sullivan Theater waiting to rehearse.
Alan Jardine, Mike Love, Carl Wilson and Bruce Johnston**

**Backstage at the Ed Sullivan Theater waiting to rehearse.
Carl Wilson, Mike Love, Alan Jardine and Bruce Johnston**

**Backstage at the Ed Sullivan Theater waiting to rehearse.
Mike Love and Dennis Wilson**

**Backstage at the Ed Sullivan Theater waiting to rehearse.
Carl at the drums. I have no idea why.**

On board John Mecom's 4-engine Viscount touring in Canada
Mike Love and wife, Susan, some time before Mike sued for divorce.

On board John Mecom's 4-engine Viscount touring in Canada
Alan Jardine and Ron Prince of The Pickle Brothers

Alan Jardine and Bruce Johnston being interviewed on local television in Edmonton, Canada.

Carl and Alan on stage in their new "uniforms" during the Canadian tour.

The Pickle Brothers comedy team during the Canadian tour.

Equipment manager and cousin to the Wilsons, Steve Korthoff with
Road Manager Dick Duryea (son of actor Dan Duryea, seated)
outside the venue between shows in Boise, Idaho at the end of
our Canadian tour.

Me, in my windowless office at the Beach Boys Ivar Avenue office. Actually, there were no windows anywhere in our offices.

Rehearsal at the University of Oklahoma in Norman, OK.
Bruce Johnston, who played electric bass as well as keyboards

**Rehearsal at the University of Oklahoma in Norman, OK.
Carl running the rehearsal.**

**Rehearsal at the University of Oklahoma in Norman, OK.
Alan Jardine and Bruce Johnston**

Rehearsal at the University of Oklahoma in Norman, OK. Billy Hinsche, Carl's brother in law, sitting in for Mike Love who was snow-bound in India.

The second of three new publicity pictures showing their new image.

Daryl Dragon at the piano before he became the Captain of the Captain and Tenille, with bass player Eddie Carter.

Waiting in the hotel lobby in Columbus, Ohio for limousines to take us to the airport. Everyone looks tired after a long night of partying after the concert. Mike Love looking upset probably because his "date" for the night said no.

Waiting in the hotel lobby in Columbus, Ohio for limousines to take us to the airport. Everyone looks tired after a long night of partying after the concert. Carl Wilson

Bruce Johnston

Alan Jardine

The mens' room that passed for our "dressing room" in Charlotte, North Carolina. Alan Jardine

Carl Wilson

Carl and Mike

Mike Love creates a "fashion shoot" in our dressing room . . . the men's room in Charlotte. I have no idea who invited her in, but no one invited her out.

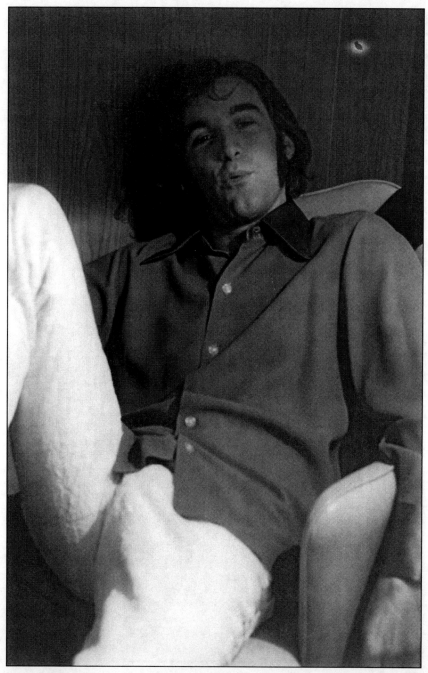

In the "Green Room" waiting around for hours with nothing to do
before being called to the stage for the *Kraft Comedy Hour.*
Dennis Wilson

Bruce Johnston

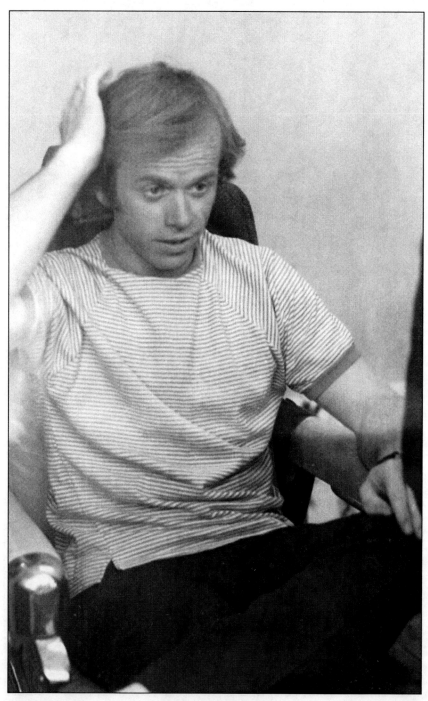

Alan Jardine

Mike Love

Don Adams dressed for a comedy skit, presumably a parody of the movie, *Golden Boy*, judging by the violin on the table for *The Kraft Comedy Hour*.

On stage filming the first of two songs as guest stars on *The Kraft Comedy Hour.*

Dover, Delaware on stage at the State Fair, where I had gone to supervise the sale of the new Beach Boy posters.
Alan Jardine

Carl Wilson

Alan, Mike (in the background), Bruce and Eddie Carter, our bass player

Carl Wilson and Mike Love

Bruce Johnston

View from my 45th floor room in Manhattan, which was supposed to be above the noise.

Could my "quiet room" be any closer to the construction?

CHAPTER THIRTEEN:
Settling into My New Routine

The first thing I did when I returned to Los Angeles and The Beach Boys' new offices on Ivar Street in Hollywood was to set about putting my office together. After all, as the new head of American Productions, I did need a place to work. The empty office next to Dick's seemed the logical place, because we could then share a secretary. Jon Parks, a sort of jack-of-all-trades around the office and on the road and I went out to a surplus office furniture store in West Los Angeles. I was looking for ways to save them money, but Jon kept finding ways to spend it. If I found something for little money, Jon found a better something for more. I finally ended up with a very nice used desk, but more importantly, a new, very expensive, and comfortable orthopedic desk chair on wheels, which incidentally, Jon took with him a few years later when *he* left The Beach Boys.

We hired a secretary, Margaret Adler, who was not only beautiful, but very efficient. I think Dick and I picked her for her looks and we were happily surprised when she turned out to be good, too. I had developed a concert work sheet for myself while I was with Irving, which I modified a little so Margaret could use it to handle all the details of promotion from the office while I was on the road. All she had to do was follow the order of "things to do" on the chart, send out the indicated publicity releases, which I had written already, on the indicated dates to the designated newspapers, and make whatever follow-up telephone calls I required.

The Beach Boys office occupied the entire second floor of a building a couple of blocks from the world-famous intersection of Hollywood and Vine, just south of Hollywood Boulevard. In addition to my office and Dick's at the back of the building, there was a bookkeeping office and a very large and expensively furnished office for Nick Grillo, the Business Manager. Nick's office had an electric door that was just like an automatic garage door, but which opened and closed sideways instead of up and down. Without the remote opener, no one could get in when he was away or didn't want to be disturbed. We all speculated on what he was doing when he closed the door. A few months later, we came up with a very accurate guess.

In addition to Margaret, Dick, and me, there were three other staff members: Nick's secretary, Lynette, who was stationed just outside his door, and the bookkeepers, Kathy and Pat.

Because all the offices were located at the back of the floor, any visitor had to walk the full length of the hallway past a room on the right with a piano, and on the left, a sauna with a shower and a storage area for original tapes and tracks, many of which had never been recorded as finished songs. The sauna and shower were hardly ever used, except by Dennis and an occasional guest, always of the opposite sex.

For reasons which will become apparent later, I will mention that Dick and Kathy were dating. All of us except Nick got to be very good friends and eventual allies.

GRILLO SHOWS HIS TRUE COLORS

As time went by, it became obvious to me that Nick lied about the contract I asked for and was promised. It was never forthcoming, and neither were the raises I expected. Nick told our staff and The Beach Boys that we were always short of money and that the company couldn't afford it. There may have been some germ of truth in that, but it didn't stop Nick from spending money whenever he wanted and for whatever reason he wanted, frequently on lunches, dinners, and motel rooms in town for himself.

I know all about libel and slander, and I also know "truth" is a defense. My information about the meals and motels came directly from conversations with Nick, which he would vigorously deny if questioned. Nick often asked me to join him for lunch, and on those occasions, he insisted on paying. I presume he did the same for Dick when I was on the road.

I told him it embarrassed me when he always paid and that I would like to pay my own way. If he had said, "No, it's okay because I make a lot of money, I would have let him, but when he said, "It's okay, I take it out of petty cash. The Beach Boys pay for it," I decided to stop eating with him.

With regard to motels, more than once, he asked me to go to dinner with him, get a couple of hookers, and go to a motel in east Hollywood, a place where, he said, he was well-known. We wouldn't even have to register. For a lot of reasons, not the least of which was that I was happily married, I never took him up on it.

At that time, Dennis was on an allowance of $100 a week, which he invariably spent or gave away within a couple of days. Then, he showed up in Nick's office, usually on Monday because he got his money on Friday, to ask for more. Nick said, "no," and Dennis backed him against the wall and demanded it. Nick, of course, always gave in.

Once I was fully settled into my office, there were two projects I wanted to get at immediately. The first was to get new publicity pictures for The Beach Boys. We were still using pictures of them wearing red and white striped shirts, but I wanted something more current. They were appearing on stage in crushed-velour suits, and the "new" image was what I needed for promotion. Gordon Green, who designed souvenir books for Irving Granz, suggested using Gene Howard, one of the city's finest commercial photographers. He and Gordon were at that time partners in a graphics firm, which may have had something to do with his recommendation. Gene was, however, one of the top commercial photographers in the business, and he did a great job.

BACK TO AND WITH THE MAHARISHI

The second item on the agenda involved Dick to a great degree. He and I set about getting ready for the Maharishi/Beach Boy tour. Dick made the hotel and transportation arrangements and I worked with the papers, radio stations, and promoters. All we had to do was get the Maharishi to join us in New York. That was the job of Mike Love, Dick, and Nick Grillo.

The first seven or eight dates were already firm, with others being finalized. Several more promoters with whom the New York agent were still negotiating assured us that they had ample time to pull everything together for perhaps another five or six east coast performances.

Then, our troubles started. Suddenly, the Maharishi was nowhere to be found, with less than ten days until the first date. After a series of frantic telephone calls, Dick managed to track him down in, I believe, Tel Aviv, where he was involved in making a movie of some kind. Nick and Dick flew ahead to New York to await the arrival of the Maharishi, while I stayed in Los Angeles finalizing some aspects of the tour.

I had to operate on the presumption that Dick and Nick would work it out, so I went ahead with my plans for the dates leaving the problem of the Maharishi to them, and possibly to Mike, who was, after all, the main reason we were featuring the Maharishi in the first place. They finally found the Maharishi, and it was finally agreed that he and the film producers would fly to New York in ample time for the first date. Nick and Dick arrived in New York ahead of me and arranged for the chartered airplane that would carry us to some of the dates too far to drive comfortably. I got to New York in time for the three of us to meet with the film's producers. Several hours of not very pleasant negotiations resulted in an agreement that the Maharishi would be in New York for appearances on the east coast where promoters had already expended considerable money. The threat of a lot of bad publicity for both the movie and the Maharishi brought the discussions to an end.

After the east coast appearances, the Maharishi could then fly back to Tel Aviv, or wherever, finish work on the movie, and return for the later west coast dates. That would have been fine with us.

The Maharishi did fly in on time and we all met at the Port Authority landing area in the airplane chartered by The Beach Boys. We were going to fly out almost immediately from there to the first date.

To prepare for my own meeting with him, I bought the Maharishi's book, which was then on the *New York Times* Bestseller List, and I finished it on my flight east. The Maharishi was accompanied by Jerry Jarvis and Charles Lutes, one the head of the students' organization, and the other the head of the international organization. Before any of us were allowed access, the Maharishi was settled into a spacious part of the main cabin that had been reserved for him. The Beach Boys were on board first, one at a time, and were each presented love beads and, I suppose, some words of wisdom before my turn came.

My conversation dealt primarily with business, as certain details had to be explained, and I was pretty much in charge of the events from there on in. However, we also spoke about his book and my feelings and disagreements with regard to his religious philosophy.

He answered that my agreement or disagreement with his religious beliefs or personal philosophy was entirely immaterial as far as TM was concerned. He was more interested in promoting Transcendental Meditation for the good of the world than in seeking religious converts.

He reasoned that if everyone in the world found inner peace through his method of meditation, there would be much less likelihood of wars. Well, I certainly couldn't argue with that. I asked him how he planned to get "everyone in the world" to meditate, and he answered, logically enough, "one person at a time." We spoke for perhaps twenty minutes with The Beach Boys sitting close enough to overhear us.

When the Maharishi and I finally finished kicking around our philosophical differences, and I went up front to where everyone else was sitting, Carl Wilson said to me, "You can't talk that way to him. It's disrespectful."

I said, "I wasn't being disrespectful at all. We were just having an intellectual discussion."

"Well, all the same, you shouldn't talk that way."

"Carl," I said, "the man is just a man. He's a bright man and he's got something to sell. He's a pitchman, with a very good pitch. I respect him for his honesty, but he's not god." Actually, I was going to finish the conversation with, "I am," but decided against it because Carl did not really have a very swift sense of humor.

Dick reserved suites for the Maharishi and his retinue—Jerry and Charlie—at the Plaza Hotel, where his rooms faced Central Park.

Dick was staying next door at St. Moritz, The Beach Boys were at the Delmonico, a hotel they liked because it had very large rooms, and I was at the Navarro on the other side of Sixth Avenue, which was also known as Avenue of the Americas. I chose the Navarro because they had a great steak house, and when I ordered a Jack Daniels and water, they put the whole bottle and water on the table.

The routine was to be pretty much the same for each performance and for each day of his stay in New York. The Maharishi would have time during the day to meet with his local followers, rest until we either flew on the charter or drove to the gig, and then return to The Plaza for the evening. He ate all his meals in the suite, as did Jerry and Charley, who didn't want to be very far away.

Even though there was considerable work left to do, Dick and I set aside some time for relaxation and to have an occasional drink at the sidewalk cafe at the corner of Avenue of the Americas, across from Central Park, where we could ogle girls.

Lynn, the secretary with whom I had been working at the agent's office, asked if I wanted her to get a date that evening for Dick, and I assured her he wouldn't mind. The four of us would meet in the lobby of the St. Moritz and have a couple of drinks.

Dodie Smith, his date, was an English girl, who had immigrated first to Canada and then to the United States where she worked in public relations. In England, she worked for the BBC. She later moved to California, got married in producer David Geffen's home, eventually divorced, and then moved back to Canada and worked with the CBC. Incidentally, the day before the nuptials, Geffen informed Dodie that he was calling off the wedding at his home. He was just being bitchy, of course. Dodie backed him against the wall (essentially and possibly figuratively) and told him in no uncertain terms that the wedding would proceed as planned and that was all there was to that. It was a lovely affair, and David, who would eventually become part of a major film company, was nice to everyone.

After a few drinks, Dick invited us all to his room to see the view. I knew he was in a single, and even though it was an old line, Dick wasn't the type to take three other people to his room for some ulterior motive; one, maybe, but not three.

The room was so small that you wouldn't even *want* to entertain in it, let alone try it with four people, no matter how friendly they were. With a flourish, he pulled back the drapes to reveal—a brick wall. His "view" was the hotel next door. You couldn't even get air through his window.

I GET INITIATED

Because The Beach Boys were so involved with TM, I decided it wouldn't be a bad idea if I was initiated into it, as well. As TM was Hollywood's current fad, I couldn't help knowing something about it. The Beatles talked about it all the time. Many of Hollywood's glitterati espoused its virtues in print and on television, and I had even once attended an orientation meeting, so I figured I already knew enough, except of course, how to do it.

The Maharishi agreed to do the initiation himself in his bedroom at the Plaza. I really didn't relish the idea of going to any more indoctrination meetings and listening to sales pitches, particularly in New York where finding the time would have been next to impossible. What's more, I didn't want to pay the $75.

The morning of the "big event" arrived and I prepared myself with a new handkerchief. I actually had some with me, but needed to make a stop for the rest of the items that would be required for the initiation. I went down into the subway, stopped at a couple of vendors there, and purchased a large, ripe, Delicious apple and some fresh flowers. The initiation had to be in the morning because we had a considerable drive to a performance that afternoon.

I entered the bedroom to find the guru sitting up in bed, reading. He greeted me warmly and we spoke for about ten or fifteen minutes about Transcendental Meditation and philosophy in general, and then he called Charley Lutes to come in and perform the ritual.

Charley took my handkerchief, the flowers, and the apple, and he led me to a small table near a window that overlooked Central Park. *A lovely view to go with the ceremony*, I thought. He arranged the handkerchief with the apple on top of the table, in front of a picture of the Maharishi's guru, and then spread the flowers around. All in all, with the view out the window and everything, it made for a very nice effect.

Charlie began chanting in Sanskrit, Hindi, or whatever (I don't claim to know the minutiae of TM), and I tried to take it all seriously, actually doing quite well until he started throwing rice at the picture. I swear that's what he did. I managed to maintain a serious demeanor, which I thought was a tribute to my powers of self-control.

Having completed the ceremony, I returned to the Maharishi's bedside, where he asked me a couple more questions and had me lean in to him while he whispered into my ear.

I said, "What?" I had no idea what he said because he spoke very softly, didn't actually say a real word, and I wasn't sure I heard it right. He repeated it, and I said, "Okay," still having no idea what he was talking about.

Charley ushered me from the bedroom, across the living room and to another bedroom, where I was to have my practice meditation. I asked, "What did he say?"

Charley said, "He gave you a personal mantra. You do remember what he said, don't you?"

"Sure," I said, and started to repeat it to him.

He said very quickly, "You must never tell your mantra to anyone other than your teacher."

I said that was fine with me, figuring there were probably only five or six mantras anyway, and they didn't want people comparing notes—or mantras—because they might find out that every sixth or seventh person had the same one. *What the hell*, I thought, *I'm only doing this for business, so I'll just go along with the gag.*

Charley explained that I didn't have to clear my mind or concentrate on my navel or do anything but say my mantra silently over and over again and fill my mind with the sound of the mantra. I was to try to avoid getting into any particular rhythm, and not to worry if I found myself drifting into thoughts other than my mantra. As soon as I realized I wasn't doing the mantra, all I had to do was start over again. That entire procedure was to last thirty minutes, during which he would sit in the room with me, observing, but I had no idea what he was to observe.

I settled comfortably in a large chair, crossed my hands on my lap, and started my meditation. I discovered quickly that even though my head was filled with my mantra, I could hear clearly and understand everything that was going on in the next room. *Isn't that interesting*, I thought, immediately losing my mantra. *I ought to start over again and stop thinking that I've lost my train of concentration. I shouldn't be thinking about losing my concentration.*

As I seemed to get into it, I could sense my breathing and heart rate actually slow down, and I felt as though I was sinking into the chair, but then I had an odd sensation. It was as though a weight was being lifted off the top of my head. As soon as that began, I started thinking about how good it felt, and as soon as I started thinking it felt good, the good feeling left. So I had to start over, and pretty soon the good feeling started all over again. At the end of the half hour, I found myself remarkably refreshed, as though my internal batteries had undergone a quick charge.

I opened my eyes slowly, as I was instructed by Charlie, relaxed for a few seconds, checked the time, and went into the living room to get the Maharishi away from a group of about fifty followers sitting at his feet hanging on his every word.

I accompanied him into the bedroom, essentially to hustle him along because the Maharishi never did anything in a hurry. I thought of the old Negro League pitcher, Satchel Paige, and *his* philosophy of never doing anything in a rush to "avoid janglin' the juices." I thought, *Satchel and the Maharishi would have liked each other.*

By then, it was close to lunch time. Since I was hungry, I stopped at the little table where I left my apple and took it back. I walked out into the living room eating it, to the accompaniment of a chorus of gasps from the assembled throng. You would have thought I committed the original sin—or worse.

In the freight elevator down to the car, I asked the Maharishi what he did with the fruit people brought him. "I eat it," he said, "or give it away."

"Do you have any objection to my eating it?" I asked.

"Of course not. If someone doesn't, the fruit will go to waste and *that* would be a sin."

I also told him of my experience with the practice session and asked if that was the sort of thing I should feel. He answered, "It's a good start." On the ride, I asked him more about TM—partly because I was going to be moderating the press conferences, and he explained, "Just think of TM as a tool, and like any other tool, you use it if it works for you. If it doesn't work, don't use it. All I want people to do is try it. One of the best things about TM is that once you've done it, you're an expert."

Although The Beach Boys did perform, I hate to call it a performance. On the way back, Jerry, Charlie, and I joined the Maharishi in his limousine. I sat in the front seat next to the driver while Jerry and Charley used the rear "jump seats," leaving the entire back seat to the guru, who sat on his deer skin, which Jerry and Charlie fought for the right to carry.

The Maharishi must have a very tender ass, if he always has to sit on a deer skin. A few minutes later, I looked back and saw him seated cross-legged, seemingly deep in meditation. *Boy, that's terrific, the way he can just get into it.* I did a lot of thinking because there was no sense in trying to get Charley or Jerry into any sort of conversation.

When we arrived at the hotel and got back to his suite, I said, "It's amazing the way you can go into deep meditation so quickly, especially in a moving vehicle." He said, "I wasn't meditating, I was sleeping. I don't meditate *all* the time, you know."

Charlie and Jerry went wherever I went, never more than a few feet away, making sure, I imagine, that the Maharishi and I didn't get too chummy. I guess they were worried about their jobs.

A few days later, after watching those two adults acting like little children and fighting for his attention, I cautioned the Maharishi that Charlie and Jerry were doing their best to deify him. "You know what happens to people who try to play god, don't you? They end up hanging on a cross." He assured me that I had nothing to worry, that he watched them closely, and that he would never let it happen.

TM DOESN'T ALWAYS SOLVE PROBLEMS

An interesting and unexpected thing with TM happened while we were still in New York. One night, I was very restless and it was getting very late. I couldn't fall asleep and even television couldn't put me out. *What the heck*, I figured, *I'll relax when I meditate and I'll give it a try.* Back then, we were supposed to meditate for thirty minutes, so I dutifully did my time and came out of it relaxed. I stretched out on the bed and closed my eyes again, fully expecting sleep to follow quickly.

Wrong. Never had I experienced anything like it, and never, I assure you, since. I saw colors that no painter ever saw, not even Van Gogh. They swirled around me like an acid freak-out, or what I imagined one would be like. My brain felt like it was on fire. I opened my eyes and it went away. I tried again and the same thing happened, and so I spent the entire night sitting up watching television. The next morning, the Maharishi explained that one must never meditate after eating or before sleeping because it creates too much energy. I had to agree with him.

Wherever possible, the performances were coupled with a press conference, either before or afterward. At Georgetown University in Washington, DC, there was a particularly obnoxious newsman standing in the back of the room, interrupting other reporters with particularly stupid questions, aimed primarily at embarrassing the guru. I was starting to get a little pissed, and as I was acting as moderator, I said something to him.

The Maharishi turned to me and said quietly, "Don't worry about him. Just ask him to meet me after the conference." I did, and I found that he didn't need my help with anyone. First of all, you must understand that the Maharishi was a well-educated and very intelligent man, a university graduate, and could handle himself in any situation. Whatever opinion you may have of the Maharishi, I can honestly say that he impressed the hell out of me.

Other than Georgetown, only one other date really stands out in my memory. We were booked into the Spectrum in Philadelphia, a huge arena that held perhaps 20,000 people. I worried about the location from the time they told me about it, but I called the promoters and insisted, "You can't set this up in the round. I want people to be able to see him."

When we arrived, we found that the promoters had indeed put the stage in the middle of the arena floor, more like a boxing ring without the ring posts and ropes, and they were selling cheaper seats in the back. It seemed to us that the people in the back were mostly college students, the group the Maharishi wanted to reach. As I mentioned a little earlier, he believed that through TM, students would be able to learn more quickly and retain more information.

He explained to me that the more one used TM, the easier it became; that people reached the ability to meditate for as much as twenty-four hours straight. My personal opinion was that they had fallen asleep and woke up twenty-four hours later, but the point wasn't worth arguing. Through personal experience, I can attest that TM does work as advertised; at least it did for me and a great many people with whom I subsequently spoke or shared a group meditation.

At the Spectrum, Dick and I agreed that because our sound system would be set up behind The Beach Boys, we would have to do something or the people sitting behind the stage would be completely shut out from the Maharishi and The Beach Boys. Even though we knew the promoters would be upset, I went out onto the stage and asked everyone in the back to move up and find seats in front. The promoters, as expected, went slightly ballistic. What was going to happen if people asked for their money back because they had paid more for their seats? So, I went back out and announced that if anyone was unhappy, they could go to the box office right then and get a refund, but that once The Beach Boys started, all bets were off. Only one person asked for a refund.

When The Beach Boys finished the first half, I announced a short intermission. I served essentially as an emcee for those dates only because no one else wanted to do it, least of all Charley or Jerry, while the crew cleared the stage and re-dressed it for the Maharishi. The stage for him was bare except for a riser where the drums had been, and on which his deer skin was set. Flowers were strewn all around him and around the stage.

I asked him why he wanted the flowers, which cost us a lot of extra money.

He said, "Because they are pretty and they smell nice."

He was a much less complicated man than people presumed. Once everything was ready to go, I started the second half and Mike Love joined me on the stage behind the Maharishi where we could listen to the lecture, which I hadn't found time to do until then.

Mike said, "Why don't we try meditating while he's talking, just to see what happens?"

I said, "Okay, why not."

I know that sounds like crap, but something did happen and it happened to both of us. We sat there meditating and listening. Remember I said that while you meditate you are totally aware of what is happening around you. Words just go inside your head even while you're silently repeating your mantra. As he spoke, we both experienced the feeling of waves of pressure bouncing back against our chests. I have no idea what that means, but it did happen.

One morning, because we didn't have a performance that day, I walked over to The Plaza to meet Dick for breakfast in The Palm Court at the Plaza, an open area surrounded by little palm trees in the lobby of the hotel, where I had once been refused service because I wasn't wearing a tie. I was wearing a suit and a silk turtleneck dress shirt, which was all the rage back then. I explained that a tie with a turtleneck would be silly.

They said, "Sorry, no tie, no eat," or words to that effect.

That morning, I wore a tie with a turtleneck dress shirt.

Dick came down and said, "We've got problems."

The Maharishi, through Jerry and Charlie, informed Nick that he was not well. He was so ill, he said, he would have to return to Tel Aviv, or wherever, immediately. I suggested that he try using TM to make himself better, but I was ignored. Nick and Dick insisted he see a doctor before he did anything rash. He finally agreed, but only if the doctor was involved in TM. We figured we were pretty much dead right there, but he agreed to make one more appearance on the following day. After that, he was definitely going home.

There was nothing we could do or say that would change his mind. Charley and Jerry said the doctor insisted he return home to rest and that his health made it impossible to continue. There were only two or three dates left in the east and he could have gone home then as originally planned, but they were adamant. In fact, airplane reservations had already been made. Personally, I think the only reason they agreed to that one more date was that they couldn't get reservations any earlier. We held a meeting and decided that suing him would be a waste of time, especially if he was already back in

India or Israel. "How would it seem," we agreed, "for The Beach Boys to sue their holy man?"

All that was left for us to do was call all the promoters, cancel, and offer to pay back whatever expenses they had incurred up to that time for advertising, ticket printing, and whatever else they could think up to pad the bill. We didn't argue.

CHAPTER FOURTEEN:
Expanding and Diversifying

Even though I was running the production company, it wasn't always necessary for me to go on tour with The Beach Boys. My primary function at American Productions, at least early on, after I had re-arranged the *Million Dollar Tour* of the south, was to set up and promote the dates. Sometimes, because of where I finished my second promotion trip, it was easy for me to pick up the tour and go on with them. Then, too, when the William Morris Agency booked enough dates, there wasn't always a reason for me to be on the road. Dick Duryea was fully capable of running the day-to-day details and the box office, although I later learned that he was not very good at doing math, never, however, to our detriment.

I say that my job was to "set up" dates. More specifically, we would decide that it was time to be out in public, in front of the people who bought their records and to make new fans. Staging concerts increased record sales, and record sales made concerts more profitable. It would have been too risky for us to finance all our own concerts, and so The William Morris Agency booked us for some guaranteed income. I did, however, occasionally travel to dates we sold. Dick, on the other hand, went to *every* concert both here and abroad. As Road Manager, that was his function, and he was good at it.

Setting up a concert began with deciding where we wanted to travel. It doesn't take a lot of imagination to figure that we went where record sales and radio air play were best. Of course, we couldn't keep going back to the same places every few months, although there were some cities we could, and did, play very profitably every six months or so, like Columbus, Ohio, which meant we had to find more and more locations. Some of those places were cities that had never seen a major rock and roll concert, at least until we went there. Like St. Johns, New Brunswick, Canada.

We looked for places that could accommodate anywhere from 400 to 4,000 people, doing two shows at smaller halls. Back in 1968 when I joined them, The Beach Boys were not at the peak of their popularity. They were put down by reviewers and some of the flower-power generation for not being relevant; for not having a message. I claimed The Beach Boys did have a message: it was still okay to have a good time.

So, we had to be satisfied to a large degree playing smaller, more intimate venues to hardcore fans in cities like Akron and Canton, Ohio; Anderson, Indiana; Augusta, Georgia (a sold date); colleges like VPI (now known as Virginia Tech) and RPI; Bangor, Maine; Boise, Idaho; Charleston, West Virginia; Davenport and Des Moines, Iowa: Daytona Beach, Tampa, Sarasota, and Orlando, Florida; Fargo and Minot, North Dakota; Hartford, Connecticut, and Providence, Rhode Island, to name a few.

Of course, there were a great many locations where we had a huge following and always drew big crowds like Boston, Massachusetts; Miami Beach and Jacksonville, Florida; Atlanta, Georgia; Cleveland and Columbus, Ohio; Dallas and Houston, Texas; Louisville, Kentucky; Honolulu, Hawaii; every major city in Canada; Japan, and everywhere in Europe.

SOMETHING NEW IN PROMOTION

A few months after I left Irving for The Beach Boys, a group calling itself the Independent Promoters Association formed and we felt it would be a good idea for us to join because we were, after all, promoters, albeit of our own dates, but promoters nevertheless. The very first meeting was held in Houston, Texas, and it was decided that I should attend to see what I might learn from the "old timers."

I checked into the meeting and set about introducing myself to the other promoters, many of whom I knew from telephone conversations while I was still with Irving. People like Ralph

Bridges and Henry Wynn of Atlanta, and the legendary Lon Varnell of Tracy City, Tennessee. "Mr. Lon" bought up to fifteen Lawrence Welk dates a year, and when Andy Williams and Henry Mancini toured, he bought three or four of those, and he bought The Beach Boys for Nashville. Although we sold the date to Mr. Lon, he insisted I come to Nashville to work with him on promoting the date. He dragged me to newspapers, radio stations, a couple of television stations, and around the city to help him post handbills, pretty active for a man already in his seventies. He also took me to meet the Lieutenant Governor, who made me an Honorary Sergeant-At-Arms in the Tennessee Legislature and loaded me down with things like cuff links and tie bars all bearing the State seal.

Some of the other legendary promoters I met on the telephone were people like X. Cosse from Nashville, Barry Fey from Denver, Jerry Nathan from Buffalo, Frank Fried from Chicago, and the Belkin brothers, Mike and Jules, from Cleveland.

As the meeting was called to order, I took a seat in the front row because I didn't want to miss any pearls of wisdom that might drop from the mouths of those promoters, all with years more experience than I. The Association President opened the meeting and introduced me to the group, because in addition to being a promoter, I also represented talent. I was the only person at the meeting who could speak from both sides of the contract. I stood up to acknowledge the introduction and sat down quickly to wait for the first speaker.

The President said, "Why don't we ask Jack to be our first speaker?"

I tried to wave him off, but he wouldn't hear of it.

The other promoters said, "Go on up."

Having no idea what I was going to say had never stopped me before, so I went to the podium and began talking about what it was like to promote our own shows and to sell the act to other promoters. I guess I managed about ten or fifteen minutes before I ran out of anything intelligent to say. Being stuck, I did the obvious thing: I asked if there were any questions.

I was stunned at the number of hands that shot in the air. Those people, from whom I came to learn, apparently wanted to learn from me. One of the first questions I fielded was, "What percentage of your budget do you allocate to radio or newspaper advertising?" Now that was a question I thought everyone would know the answer to, but I was wrong because it opened a twenty-minute discussion. Then, someone asked about how much we allowed ourselves for buying second or third acts, and how did I scale certain houses.

The questions were so basic, I got to wondering how those people were such successful promoters, and they were . . . all of them. I was comparatively a neophyte, but there I was telling those people what I was positive any of them would and should have known.

A LITTLE MISCELLANY

In 1965, when I joined Irving Granz, I grew a beard to which I became very attached, as it did to me. At first, I wore it in a Van Dyke cut, but during a trip with Andy Williams, his manager, Alan Bernard, who also wore a beard that was cut very close, said: "Hey, beard, why don't you grow it full, like mine?"

As soon as I got home, I asked my daughter whether I should keep it in a Van Dyke or grow it full. She voted for full and it's been that way ever since, although I do keep it trimmed moderately close.

Pretty soon, Nick Grillo decided he didn't like my beard and ordered me to remove it. In words a little stronger, I told him to forget it; the beard was part of me. He then issued another proclamation that Dick and I had to wear a necktie every day. I wore one, but as soon as I saw him, I immediately loosened it and it remained that way.

One day, Carl dropped into the office and said, "Hey, Jack, I really dig your beard," and immediately began growing one himself. The next time he was in the office, he was sporting a full brush. Very soon after that, Nick grew a beard and that was the end of that conversation.

Nick had some other peculiar habits, but one in particular bears mentioning. He kept in his desk drawer an 11x14 photograph of a very large-breasted young woman. Of course, I saw nothing wrong with that, as I too, liked looking at attractive young women in less than full dress. He could have had a picture of her *naked* from the waist up, but he chose one of her wearing a bra. Oh, well, "to each his own," as they say.

CHAPTER FIFTEEN:
It Isn't Always Easy to Unclutter a Mind

A month or so before the two tours, Dick and Dennis Wilson had some kind of altercation while they were in Florida. I heard sketchy details only from Nick, but as I understood it, Dennis got pissed at Dick while they were on someone's yacht. To quote Nick, "Dennis decked him." They sent Dick home and he took a couple of weeks off before returning to the office. All I knew was that he was taking a vacation. By the time he got back, the "why" was no longer important and things were more or less back to normal.

Mike Love had called Nick from Florida and ordered him to fire Dick. For more than one reason, Nick didn't want to do that. First of all, he was involved with Dick in some kind of a land deal for The Beach Boys through Dick's contacts. Nick expected, as I was led to believe, to get 25 percent for his work and I gathered Dick expected the same because he was going to broker the deal with his friends. For whatever reason, the land deal never came to fruition and may have been the reason Nick was eventually fired. It was probably at least one reason Dick quit shortly after I did.

Before Dick came back to the office, Nick had asked me to help him save Dick's job. I was more than willing to do it because Dick and I were friends and I certainly enjoyed our working together.

When the boys returned from Florida, Nick asked for a meeting at Mike's Coldwater Canyon home in Beverly Hills. He and I drove there together, pretty much in silence.

At the meeting, I kept waiting for Nick to say something that would get the meeting started, but he just sat there. I didn't think it was my place to instigate the conversation because I still had no idea what had generated Mike's demand that Dick be fired.

At last Mike said, "Why are we bothering with this meeting? Didn't we already fire him? We don't want him around any more."

I thought that was pretty extreme, but it still wasn't my place to say anything. I thought, *Okay, that's it, let's go home. There's obviously nothing I can do here.*

Nick finally spoke up. "Jack says he really needs Dick."

I mumbled something or other that came out that I liked Dick and thought he liked me, and when we traveled together, things seemed to always go smoothly. I saw no reason to eliminate him from the company, and yes, there was no doubt life would get more difficult for me. I added that while I couldn't say for certain, because I didn't know that many Road Managers, but from my point of view, Dick certainly seemed to be one of the best in the business. They must have felt that way once or they wouldn't have hired him in the first place.

The discussion went on for some time, mostly without comment from me, with a more or less final decision that Dick could stay, but on the condition that he never went on the road with them again. That meant I would be not only the "producer," but the Road Manager as well, and it meant I would be out of the office for longer periods of time. That part didn't concern me because there was nothing I did from the office that Dick and Margaret couldn't do while I was away, and there was always the telephone if I was needed.

It was about that time that Nick began a campaign to undermine my relationship with Dick and vice versa. He apparently told Dick that I was working to take his job, that I couldn't be trusted, and that it was the two of them against me. Of course, Dick probably never knew I had helped to save his job because I'd bet money that Nick never told him.

During the time Dick was out of the office on his "vacation" or whatever it was, Nick began working on me to turn against Dick. It was "It's you and me against Dick," or "Dick is trying to get us both fired so he can be their manager." I didn't think Dick would do anything like that, but I was getting a little concerned about my future.

I could sense a growing tension between Dick and me, although nothing overt happened, but I could feel some tension, and by then I was starting to get paranoid about getting dumped. However, I didn't run out and start looking for another job and never mentioned it to anyone in the office.

One day, Dick came into my office and suggested that we talk. Once we compared notes it was obvious what Nick was up to. I suspect that Nick realized that Dick and I were closer to the boys than he was, or he thought we were, which was just as good. He was hedging his bets in the event that either Dick or I got canned and he needed a liaison to stand up for him. In my experience, that's what people with "dirty hands" did.

When Nick realized that we were no longer at odds with one another, although we had never been less than civil, Nick issued yet another edict barring the girls in the office from having anything to do with either of us, in or out of the office. Of course, Dick went right on dating Kathy, and whenever the opportunity presented itself, Pat and I hugged and nuzzled in front of Nick's open door just to bug him.

AN UNEXPECTED CALL TO WORK

I was back in Los Angeles when I got a telephone call from Kip Cohen, an associate of famed rock promoter Bill Graham, with whom, incidentally, I never had a normal conversation. Every call, dating back to my work with Irving Granz, ended in a shouting match. Eventually, he gave a little, I gave a little, and we always worked out whatever problems we had. I'm sure that was to no one's complete satisfaction, which was why I was very surprised to get a call from Kip. He ran The Fillmore East, a converted theater in New York's East Village, the east coast counterpart to Graham's Fillmore West in San Francisco.

Kip said he wanted to book The Beach Boys, which I thought was a little nuts because I couldn't imagine the people who inhabited the East Village having any interest in them. "Don't you think we're the wrong act for the Fillmore?" I asked.

The Fillmore East generally showcased acts like Janis Joplin, Country Joe and the Fish, the Sheep, The Chocolate Telephone Pole, Vanilla Fudge, maybe Steppenwolf or Tommy James and the Shondells, and The Jefferson Airplane. Patrons of both Fillmores were largely culled from the east and west coast "hippies" and pot heads.

Kip assured me that we'd do well and made an offer the size of which surprised me. The place was not really large enough to make much of a profit without doing two shows, the second of which was always at midnight. I couldn't believe Beach Boy fans would come to the Fillmore or anywhere at midnight.

Kip insisted he knew what he was doing and questioned who I was to disagree. After all, it was his place.

I said, "The money is terrific, but I'm going to have to talk this over with Dick." I promised to get back to him within twenty-four hours. I hung up and walked to Dick's office. "You're not going to believe the call I just had," I said, relating the details of Kip's offer. "What do you think? Should we do it or do you think the Boys will be embarrassed?"

Dick agreed the offer was so good it would be very hard to refuse, and we decided it was worth a try. I called Kip and told him to go ahead and send a contract. We went to Nick and told him what we had just done. He was very enthusiastic because it gave him an excuse to go back to New York and visit the hookers in Spanish Harlem on company money.

Nick was married to a very beautiful young woman, also a New Yorker, who wanted to go back east with him for the show. She asked if he would take her, but Nick, every bit the loving husband, told her, "If you want to go back, get a job and buy your own ticket."

None of us knew of their conversation until she showed up unexpectedly at the Fillmore during rehearsal. I can't recall her name, so let's call her Linda, too. It's such a nice name and she *was* pretty, so it fits. I do remember that everyone liked her and were delighted to include her in *our* party plans, if not Nick's.

Carl asked what she was doing in New York and she related Nick's comment about her going to New York with us. She did just what Nick suggested. She went out and got a job, earned enough money for the trip, and flew east on her own. She was planning to spend part of her time visiting and staying with friends and family and had no intention of spending any time with her husband.

We insisted she hang out with us, see the show from back stage, and come to dinner afterwards. I think we all had a kind of secret lust for her; she was that beautiful.

While The Beach Boys were rehearsing, I walked outside to look around and was soon joined by Nick. We stopped passersby and asked them, "What do you think about The Beach Boys doing a show here?" One young man dressed in a flowing cape and a large floppy beret replied, succinctly enough, "Weird, man."

I met with Kip, who was not at all unhappy even though they had not yet sold out either of the two shows.

"Don't worry. You just don't know our audiences. We'll sell 25 percent of the house at the walk up. The late show is *always* a sell out.

He was right. The window sale was intense, and if they didn't completely sell out, it was pretty damn close, contrary to David Leaf's comments in his 1978 book about The Beach Boys. He reported the show as a flop. He was wrong.

What really surprised me was the audience reaction, particularly at the end of the second show. By the time The Beach Boys launched into their finale, a medley of "Barbara Ann" and "Sloop John B," the place was rocking. I mean, the people were dancing in the aisles. In the steep balcony where I went to watch the end of the show, they were standing on the seats, bouncing up and down to the music. I was positive someone was going to bounce himself or herself right out of the balcony onto the crowd below.

That night was the first time I sent other acts onto the stage to join in the finale, something which apparently became a regular part of their performances after I left. As the other acts came out the response grew louder and louder. When Dennis came off stage and pulled someone out of the audience to dance with him, the fans went berserk. Kip Cohen was right; he knew his audience.

IT TAKES A HEAP OF DOING TO
MAKE A TOUR A TOUR

Early the next morning, I flew to Louisville, Kentucky to start promoting a long series of dates we booked through the southeast. I spent the better part of the day there, lined up twelve girls for the party after the show, and the next morning flew on to Columbus, Ohio, where we would be going in less than a month.

I checked into the International Inn and called young Jennifer, the girl who went out with Marcus Hemphill on my trip there with Andy Williams and Henry Mancini. Dolores, the girl I had taken to dinner that night, was then married or soon to be married to her high school sweetheart. I kept my promise to Dolores and took sixteen-year-old Jennifer to a movie and for an ice cream soda.

The next morning, before catching an airplane to Boston, I visited the newspapers and the radio station, where one of the jocks told me the manager of the Music Hall had done something unthinkable. He booked rock and roll acts one week on either side of our date, similar to our experience in Miami Beach. Never before had they done that to anyone. There had always been at least a two-week cushion before, if not after, our show, and it was definitely affecting sales.

It was bad enough that the University of Michigan was playing their annual blood-bath-bowl football game there in Columbus that same weekend, a game which also turned out to be for the Big 10 championship and a date in the Rose Bowl on New Year's Day. There ensued a verbal, knock-down, drag-out fight with the manager of the Music Hall, the end result of which was some sort of financial concessions. There was nothing he could or would do to make either of other shows change their dates.

From Columbus, I flew into Boston to meet with Fred Taylor, who was promoting the show for us there, and spent the evening at his jazz club, Paul's Mall.

ON THE ROAD AGAIN—AGAIN

The next morning, I flew back to New York to meet The Beach Boys, who had been off somewhere doing a couple of concerts. They arrived in town around nine o'clock in the morning, just in time to catch our airplane to Knoxville, Tennessee.

It was pouring rain when we landed in Knoxville, which was always a concern when it came to ticket sales the night of the show. We checked into the Esquire Inn after collecting three or four rental cars in which we planned to make the rest of the trip because Nick thought we would save money by not flying between dates.

After settling in our rooms, some of us went to the auditorium. The Beach Boys wanted to rehearse with the horn section we added for that trip and I wanted to check the stage and the box office, as was my usual habit. Traffic was heavy in the rain and it was taking too long for us to get there. Doug Dragon was our "relief" drummer for that trip. He played the drums when Dennis was downstage singing. He was driving the car in which I was riding, and he also thought the trip was taking too long.

He decided we could get there faster if he went around traffic by driving down the center divider, which was fine with me, but it was a little nerve-wracking whenever cars in the left lane on either side of the road came close. Things were fine until the divider narrowed as we approached a stop light. Doug managed to pull back into traffic just before we ran out of concrete. I had visions of us hung up on the divider, two wheels on either side, unable to move anywhere.

The following day, after a successful show, our auto caravan started out for Greenville, South Carolina. The drive through the great Smokey Mountains was unbelievably beautiful with the clear mountain streams that were there back then, thick groves of woodland, and white water rapids. We stopped at a small inn for lunch and some of the guys went off tramping through the nearby woods on a nature hike.

Back on the road, we stopped, along with about a hundred other idiots, to ogle some bears that had wandered close to the highway looking for handouts. Even I know you're supposed to stay in your car when bears approach.

After several sight-seeing stops along the way, we arrived in Greenville. Well, some of us did.

The two cars trailing the one I was driving were stopped by the highway law enforcement officers. Dennis Wilson, who was driving the first car after ours, found a place where he wanted to stop. Oddly enough, it was the same place where we had stopped earlier, and he wanted to maybe to look at the river, or piss on a tree; who knows why Dennis did things. Anyway, there was a broken-down, abandoned building nearby and they began lobbing stones toward it, just as we had done when we stopped, I suppose to break whatever windows we left, when someone saw them and called the cops. They caught up with our vandals several miles down the road.

Dennis, unknown to me and as far as I knew, anyone else, had secured a chunk of hashish somewhere along the way. When he saw the cops signaling from behind, he panicked and instead of tossing it out the window, swallowed the whole thing. By the time they finally rolled into the hotel driveway, Dennis was pretty sick. Fortunately, the cop never suspected and Dennis almost fully recovered by show time. The cop, because Dennis begged him, called me at the hotel before dragging them all off to the clink. He wouldn't believe that Dennis was a rock star and that they were all on their way to Greenville for a show that night. I talked him into bringing everyone to the hotel where we could discuss the problem face-to-face.

By showing him an ad and a poster, I was able to make the patrolman understand that Dennis was a very important part of the show and that a lot of people in town would be very unhappy if he didn't show up that night. I promised to keep a close watch on him and not let him get into any more trouble while we were in the state, and properly chastise him.

I also promised the cop we wouldn't leave town the next day until I heard from him, and that if someone sent us a bill, we would pay for the damage our people did, if they could show us what damage we did and which damage was done before we and Dennis got there.

Finally, to get rid of him, I promised that if there was to be any fine, I would pay it—and the damages—even it I had to mail the money.

The attendance was only fair, and, according to my notes, no one was able to score with the very attractive hotel desk clerk, the only really good-looking girl around, although I think most everyone gave it a try. However, two of The Beach Boys, who shall remain nameless in the event their wives ever read this, met a couple of female fans in the parking lot later and took them to their rooms. So, at least two members of the troupe weren't totally unsatisfied.

The next morning, our band of nomads drove to Greensboro, once again through the mountains, and then directly to the auditorium.

Dennis found someone with a go-kart and went spinning around the parking lot, but the concert was uneventful. Dennis actually ran into a couple of girls he knew or claimed to know from somewhere. He told one of them she could go with us to the next stop if she agreed to give Al head, but she didn't like Al and wouldn't do it.

So Dennis took her off into a shower in the dressing room where she gave *him* head but he couldn't finish before he had to go on stage, which made him surly and less than enthusiastic during the performance. Actually, he was doing a pretty bad job, practically sleep-walking through the show.

I tried yelling at him from the wings, but he ignored me or didn't hear me. So, I took a Frisbee, one of several that we always carried with us, and threw it at him. It sailed over his head, but it got his attention. Someone on the other side of the stage threw it back, but Dennis caught it, and threw it at me. Pretty soon, he was having such a good time, he forgot to sulk and was fine the rest of the concert.

Immediately following the show, Bruce, Mike, Carl, and I decided to drive straight through to Louisville, Kentucky, our next date some 600 miles away. At the last minute, Bruce changed his mind and Dennis went instead. There was no problem, as far as the tour was concerned, with anyone leaving the next morning because we had the day off, but the four of us wanted to kick back and relax for an entire day, which we could do by driving all night.

Driving once again through the Blue Ridge Mountains was difficult because of all the twists, turns, and hairpin cutbacks in the dark, but I still managed to average close to 50-miles an hour. We finally dropped down the west side of the mountains to flat land, where we joined US 64 and could get up some speed.

It was still dark when we reached the turnpike, and I finally got so tired I could hardly keep my eyes open. I had to get some rest. Carl volunteered to drive. Dennis said, from the back seat, "Don't drive 100," a phase he mumbled several more times to me throughout the night. When I was driving, I would reply, "Don't worry Dennis, I won't drive that slow." Mike kept encouraging me to drive faster.

Anyway, Carl took the wheel and I took his place in the front seat, admonishing him not to go slower than 90 if we were to get the Louisville at a reasonable hour in the morning. I tried to sleep, but it was impossible because I could feel Carl slow down around every little turn in the road. I rested my eyes for forty-five minutes and had Carl stop to change seats with me again.

Towards dawn, we were into West Virginia, a rather poor, coal-mining state. I remember looking across a field in the cold gray light just before sunrise and seeing a ramshackle cabin next to a pond, a single light illuminating the interior, and a wisp of smoke rising straight up from the chimney. I thought, *This looks like a postcard or a painting*. Only later did I think about the poverty it represented.

Once on the turnpike, and later the open highway, I was able to keep the speed of our Mercury Marquis up between a 115 and 120-miles an hour. At least that's what the speedometer read. We arrived at the hotel driveway in Louisville, eleven hours after leaving the drive-in where we stopped for a bite before hitting the road, back in Greensboro. The rest of our group arrived much later that evening, all very tired.

SOME SMALL TOWNS ARE *REALLY* SMALL

Following a very successful date at Louisville's Freedom Hall, we left the following morning for Kingsport, Tennessee, which has some unusual memories for me. Obviously, it was a small town, but it had a large area from which to draw, and so we did well there. Everyone checked into their rooms after first trying to line up potential dates for the night.

The Pickle Brothers were with us again on that trip, and one of them, I'm pretty sure was Ron Prince, was in the first car to arrive at the hotel. He immediately met a young lady, Lynette, who for some reason decided to latch on to me when our car arrived about thirty minutes later. Perhaps she thought I was more important than some comic she'd never heard of. She eventually insisted on being my "date" at the after-concert party. I imagine she thought I was harmless, being so much older than everyone else, or maybe it was just my magnetic personality, which of course, I prefer to believe.

I no sooner hung up my bag in my room than Mike Love called. He had a problem. Somewhere along the way, he picked up an infestation of "crabs," little body lice that actually look like crabs when viewed under a magnifying glass. He asked me to find him some Blue Ointment or A-200, common remedies for the condition. Being Road Manager as well as producer on that trip, I had to handle little details like that, too.

I noticed a drug store across an empty lot adjacent to our motel and walked there with Jon Parks. I found the pharmacist and asked him for A-200.

He said, "I'm afraid I don't know what that is."

"How about Blue Ointment?"

"Don't know it."

"Well, do you have anything for crabs?"

"What?"

"Crabs. Body lice in the pubic region."

"Ugh. That's terrible. No, I don't have anything like that. People around these parts don't get body lice. That's disgusting."

We headed back to the hotel, where I ran into Lynette in the lobby. "Is there a large pharmacy somewhere in town?" There was. "Do me a favor and take me there."

We got into my rental car and she directed me to what amounted to a downtown section, where sure enough there was a large drug store. I located the pharmacist and went through more or less the same conversation, with the same result. My next stop was a large market where I made a purchase, and headed back to Mike's room.

I handed Mike the paper sack and told him that there was no A-200 or Blue Ointment in town. "Here's what you should do," I said. "First, shave off all your pubic hair and then spray yourself with what's in the bag."

He reached in the bag and pulled out a can of Raid. "It says it's good for crawling insects," I explained. "I figure that after you've shaved and sprayed, and after you come down off the ceiling, you'll probably be fine."

It must have worked because I didn't have to go shopping again.

CHAPTER SIXTEEN:
Traveling by Motor Gets More Interesting

The night of the concert in Kingsport, which was played in another outstanding high school auditorium, Dennis found a very pretty eighteen-year old part-American Indian girl named Judie, with whom he spent the night after promising her a recording career or a modeling contract, at the very least. She actually sang and had a demo. Who was going to make her a star? Me, naturally. I seemed to be responsible for his getting laid in one town after another. Not that he needed help, but he was not above getting very "Hollywood" with naive young girls. I was to have more to do with her later. I did not, however, get her a recording contract or even a modeling agent.

Early the next morning, we piled back into our cars for the drive once again to Virginia, back through the mountains, and on to Roanoke, where we checked into a hotel. We were in Roanoke because it was the closest city to our next date in Blacksburg, where there was not much other than Virginia Polytechnic Institute (VPI), now better known simply as Virginia Tech. There certainly were no suitable hotel accommodations there.

The show was good; it always is when we had a captive audience with nothing better to do and no place better to go. There was only one problem: Dennis ran into someone outside the dressing room, who gave him a hit of cocaine. He felt terrific, but his timing during the show was terrible. When he came off the stage and into the dressing room, he was all smiles. I don't know what it is with drug users in the music business. They all insist they write better songs and play better music when they're high, but I've yet to see it. Mostly, the ones I knew wrote badly and played worse on any kind of drug including marijuana.

"Boy, was I ever great tonight," he said.

Carl said, "You played like shit."

I added my two cents, "You were awful. What the hell were you on?"

"Only a little cocaine, but man, I thought I was fantastic."

I said, "Dennis, I don't give a shit what you do after a concert or when we're not working, but you will *never* do that to me again." He never did, except once, but that was after I resigned and came back to do a few more special dates for them.

After the show, we drove back to Roanoke, where I was surprised to find Dennis's Indian girlfriend, Judie, and her friend, Kay, waiting for him and our semi-regular bass player, Eddie Carter. They flew in as a surprise, and that night, Eddie got his own room because, as a rule, our hired musicians shared rooms. Mike, Bruce, Steve Korthoff, and I, having failed to make any kind of connections for the evening, went out for pizza and talked until four o'clock in the morning.

In the morning, we headed back into and through the mountains to Charleston, West Virginia. Dennis still had his Indian with him, but Kay returned to Kingsport, at Eddie's expense, not ours.

While we were in Charleston, Mike, Bruce, and I went driving into the mountains looking for antiques. Mike found an early American buttermilk churn, which I eventually flew back to Los Angeles as my "seat mate," just as I had done for Chastity Bono's stuffed doll.

AN UNEXPECTED GLITCH IN TRAVEL PLANS

It turned out that we had a serious problem out of Charleston because our next date was in Columbus, Georgia. Originally, we thought it was drivable, but we realized that it would have been impossible for us to drive all night and be ready for an afternoon show in Columbus, even if we could get away immediately after the show. Not that we couldn't have made it in time, but they would have arrived with no rest or sleep before they had to go on stage and there was always the question of three or four rental cars getting there at the same time. I was nominated to find another way to get us there.

The William Morris Agency sold the Charleston date to Gary and Phil Lashinsky, who's National Shows produced a great many concerts in addition to the Lippanzer Stallions. Marv Lashinsky, brother to Gary and Phil, but sort of the black sheep of the family and therefore the most fun, said, "Don't worry about a thing. I can get you an airplane and you can fly to Columbus."

"How much?" said I. "Not over $600." I told The Beach Boys of Marv's offer.

They said in essence, "Go for it."

Of course, he couldn't produce an airplane for $600 or for any price that would accommodate everyone, but he did come up with a bus. You might wonder how our sound system managed to stay ahead of us, particularly on that long jump. Well, we were pretty smart about that, using two complete systems and hop-scotching them.

Everyone helped load the equipment truck and we climbed aboard the bus, which was waiting in back of the theater. The bus was configured for forty-eight, except that Dennis had somehow managed to get a row of seats removed so he and Judie could lie under them on the thin mattress he found somewhere. The trip would take thirteen hours, with three rest stops where we changed drivers; there was apparently a limit to the number of miles or hours one of those charter drivers could go at a stretch. Each rest stop was also a junk food stop. Doug Dragon, our extra drummer on this trip, and Al Jardine crawled up into the luggage rack to sleep, while Bruce laid out some guitar cases on the floor of the bus, and stretched out on them. Steve Korthoff and I commandeered the front seats and he kept falling asleep on my shoulder.

I'm not sure what Dennis and his Indian might have been doing once the lights were out, but then Dennis was an innovator and Judie was seemingly in lust.

"Dennis," I said, "I really don't mind you doing this, because Judie seems like a very nice young lady, but how do you plan on getting her back home? Or did you plan on taking her with us all the way to Los Angeles?"

"We'll buy her a plane ticket."

"And who is going to pay for the ticket?" I asked.

"We will."

"Have you asked Mike or Alan or Carl how they feel about it?" I didn't include Bruce because at that time, he was still an employee.

"No, but they won't mind. Ask them for me."

I conducted a quick poll and they decided we would pay her fare back home from Columbus, but the cost would have to come out of Dennis's pay for the tour.

NOT EVERYONE IN GEORGIA IS A SOUTHERN GENTLEMAN

We pulled into Columbus at noon and drove directly to another high school, where we had been booked for an afternoon show. I managed to scout up some towels so everyone could shower. We all needed one badly. Just before the show, which was far from sold out, I gave a little pep talk, saying that just because the house wasn't full didn't mean they shouldn't give those who came to the show a performance to tell their friends about. I was emceeing and asked everyone in the house to come down close to the front, which most of them did, and with their audience virtually on top of them, The Beach Boys did one of their very best performances.

Immediately following the show, we got back on board our bus and drove to Macon, Georgia. Jon had gone ahead with the opening act, but we arrived late by about thirty minutes. The stage hadn't been set yet and we all rushed to get it ready.

We were all weary by the time the show ended in Macon, and I had troubles with the promoter, who refused to pay us the balance of our money. He blamed us because the show wasn't sold out and because we were thirty minutes late. He wasn't eager to listen to any arguments and I was just too tired to fight.

I told him, "Either have a check in Los Angeles in two days or we'll sue you, and we'll file it in Los Angeles so you'll have to answer back there, which is going to cost you a lot more money than if you just give us the rest of our dough and let us get the hell out of here."

He said, "Go ahead and sue. I'm not giving you another dime."

I replied, "You realize this is something you can't win because we lived up to our end of the contract. It isn't our fault you did a lousy promotion job and didn't sell out." Actually, my notes showed that we drew pretty well in Macon.

I was already getting on the bus, but he followed me and wouldn't shut up. I said "What do you want from me now? You didn't pay us. So just shut up and tell your lawyer to get ready to be sued. Not only that, we have a damned good press relations group, who will make sure that every act you want to book and every agent in Los Angeles you contact will know about this, so just get the fuck away from me."

I caught a flight out of Atlanta at 12:50 a.m., and I flew home via Dallas. The airplane was grounded there, and I was put up in a toilet of a motel even though I was flying first class. I do remember that motel because first of all, they made me share a room, and worst of all, there was a hole in the ceiling where someone had removed or stolen the air conditioning unit. It rained in.

CHAPTER SEVENTEEN:
It Started in Bangor

There was a trip that included, and may even have started, in Bangor, Maine, where we scheduled two shows at the high school auditorium. Their sound system was so good that we were able to send our own equipment ahead to the next date, which might have been in New Jersey. Having completed all my work in the box office the night of the show, I went out into the auditorium and was listening to "Good Vibrations," when the radio station's top jock standing next to me started shaking his head. "Don't you like it?" I asked.

"I love it," he said, "I just didn't believe anyone could do it live."

That was something that set The Beach Boys apart from virtually every other rock act in the business. Their concert performance was the same as their recorded performance. They didn't have to rely on engineering electronics to create their sound. In point of fact, the only thing that was not live in their performances of "Good Vibrations" was a piece of recorded tape called a "loop" that was used for an echo effect that lasted only a few seconds. Voices could not duplicate that.

After the concert, I was invited by the deejay to a house party. I wasn't particularly interested in going back to the hotel, Dick was no longer on the road, and I did not know what The Beach Boys were up to. I only recall that I didn't feel like going anywhere with them that night, so I accepted the invitation. It turned out that the house party wasn't much more exciting than anything that might have happened at the hotel, but at least I didn't have to worry about the party ending up in my room, which seemed to have become the norm by then.

The party started slowly enough and I was introduced around, but as everyone there seemed to be close friends, in business with one another, or had long histories, I felt a little out of place. The hostess did her best to help, but she was busy running around from guest to guest and doing a lot of dancing. Everyone there seemed to be an excellent dancer and it turned out that some of them were in fact dance teachers. They were dancing whatever kids were dancing back in the 1960s.

I never felt comfortable doing what I considered "kid" dances. After all, I had "my" music and dances from my own Chicago youth. I grew up with the Fox Trot, the Rhumba, Jitterbugging, which is called "Swing Dancing" today, the Samba, and yes, even the Waltz.

The hostess, Karen K., was obviously a wonderful dancer, and I wanted to dance with her, but was afraid she couldn't follow my "Chicago Style." I conveyed the thought to her and she said, "Let's try." She could. Boy, how she could. It was as though we had always danced together. A little while later, sitting in the kitchen, she brought out a photo album and showed me pictures of her from a year or two earlier, when she was dancing with the Radio City Music Hall Rockettes. Then, retired and back in Bangor, she ran a dancing school.

Perhaps a year later, after I left The Beach Boys, I was in Bangor with my then partner, Jerry Fox, to determine whether we could successfully promote a Ray Charles concert for a group that had hired us to produce shows for them. I introduced Karen to Jerry and they ended up more or less in love, or whatever you called a relationship between a supplier of marijuana (Jerry) and a user (Karen). Not much of a basis for real love, but it was good enough for Jerry.

When we got back to Los Angeles, he wrote her every day, called her, sent her flowers and gifts, and of course, weed. One day, he asked me if I minded if he dated her because he was in love. I replied that it wasn't up to me whether or not they dated, and besides, Karen and I were just good friends, and long distance friends at that. She finally moved to northern California and he and she spent considerable time together. I don't know why it ended, but Jerry and she had nothing else in common that I could see, and she had her own group of friends. I doubt that Jerry fit in very well.

While I was standing in the auditorium at the concert in Bangor, an attractive young girl, perhaps twenty-two years old, approached me. She introduced herself as Priscilla something-or-other and wanted to know if we'd be back east soon. I told her we would be in Boston within a few weeks.

"If I come there," she said, "would you give me a ticket?"

I said, "Sure," fully expecting that I would never hear from her again, but I did during an upcoming tour.

Following our long, exhausting tour of the southeast, I made another quick trip to put the finishing touches on a short tour that would end in Boston and be followed immediately by a concert tour of Europe. That tour was to be covered by Dick because he made a previous European tour with them and, according to Nick Grillo, knew all the venues and the promoters who bought the dates.

A WHOLE NEW EXPERIENCE IN COLUMBUS

I flew out of Los Angeles on a Sunday morning to Columbus, Ohio, to begin promotions for the short tour. I would cover all the venues and then end up meeting The Beach Boys back in Columbus, where the tour would start. I had a long meeting with the Entertainment Editor of the *Columbus Post Dispatch*, a delightful young man named John Huddy. John eventually moved on to the *Miami Herald*, where he was equally successful. I suggested to him that it might be a very nice gesture on his part if he and his college-age sweetheart could line up about twelve girls. I pulled the number out of the air, as a surprise for The Beach Boys when we came back. He could just leave them in my room.

I woke up the next morning to freezing temperatures and a city buried in snow. My rental car was almost completely covered. After clearing the snow from the windows, I got ready to drive over to Canton, pausing only long enough to drop my distance-seeing glasses and drive over them as I backed out of the parking space. I drove north to Canton, where the manager of the field house informed me the show was not doing well. I headed out to the newspaper and radio station for some extra promotion and drove to

Akron and the Holiday Inn. As there was, and possibly still is, nothing much to do in Akron, I had dinner at the hotel, watched *El Cid* on the television, read for awhile, and then to bed.

The following morning, it was even colder and there was much more snow, and I had to drive over icy roads to Cleveland, where I caught an airplane for Boston and immediately checked-in with Fred Taylor, our local promoter. Ticket sales were picking up and all signs pointed to a double sell out.

Radio station WMEX called and tried to get me to spend some more money with them, but I didn't really have any more to spend. My budget was really tight, which is one of the reasons I was using Fred Taylor. He was going to lay out any front money for me as he had in the past for Irving Granz.

I took some time out from calling on radio stations and college newspapers to have lunch with Fred. He brought along Ken Albers and Bob Flannagan of The Four Freshman, who were in town for a gig. We did the standard conversation about how The Beach Boys had copied their harmonic style, which of course was largely true. They also told me that after years of complaining that The Beach Boys had stolen their stuff, they were now including a medley of The Beach Boys' songs in their act, but still taking credit for creating the sound.

Having completed the last promotion before the start of the tour, I flew back to Columbus to meet the airplane carrying The Beach Boys. I had previously arranged for some limousines to pick up everyone for the trip to the hotel, but when I got to the airport, I discovered that their flight had been delayed for an hour.

By the time we finally cleared all the baggage and loaded everything and everyone into the cars, I was certain that even if John had been able to line up any girls, they would have long since left.

The hotel, as hotels often did, put us all on the same floor, hoping to keep any noise and insanity confined to one relatively small area and to keep our group from disturbing the other guests. Immediately after checking in and getting room keys, I had everyone stop at my room for just a minute—in the vague hope that perhaps if John had been at all successful, a few girls would be waiting. I opened the door to find not twelve, but thirteen young women, all in their twenties.

Dennis asked, "Who are these people?"

"They're for you. Not *all* for you, Dennis . . . for all of you," I said.

Dennis walked over to a dark-haired girl, Peggy, and took her by the hand.

She asked, "Where are we going?"

He replied succinctly, "We're going to my room and fuck."

A couple of years later, Peggy moved to California with her boyfriend and we talked about that night. I asked her what happened, and she repeated what I heard Dennis say.

I asked, "Why did you go with him?"

She answered, "No one ever asked me that way before, so I figured, why the hell not."

Mike Love picked a freckle-faced Irish lass with long blonde hair and green eyes—Mike loved women with long hair—and they disappeared to his room. Everyone, including our equipment men, paired off with someone.

The next night, a free night, we all went to The Bistro, the same club where I had, on a previous trip, gone to see The Pair Extraordinaire, to dance, and to see whoever was entertaining. I recall dancing with several of the girls, including Peggy and Maureen, the green-eyed blonde with long hair, who had gone off with Mike.

Mike took me aside to complain that the previous night she was lying on his bed, finally clad only in her bra and panties, but that she wouldn't let him touch her.

"What do you want me to do about it? They're not hookers. Nothing is guaranteed. Maybe she didn't like you." That night, one of The Pickle Brothers took her to his room, and the next morning had the same complaint.

I recall one blonde in particular, not her name, but just that she was very pretty and because of what she asked me. We were all hanging around the lobby in the morning waiting for the cars to come pick us up for the trip to the airport.

I was sitting in a chair against the wall, Mike was sitting cross-legged on the floor, and Dennis was lying on the floor near him. I imagined that none of them got much sleep because, after all, the girls were still there, waiting with us.

The blonde came over to me and said, "You must know a lot of doctors in Los Angeles."

"I know some. Why?"

"Do you think you might be able to get me some birth control pills?"

"Why don't you ask your own doctor? Didn't I hear you say you're divorced and have a kid?"

"I couldn't do that," she replied, "I'd be embarrassed because then he'd know I was having sex." For that I had no answer.

Just before the cars got there, Maureen, who hadn't slept with Mike or one of The Pickle Brothers, came over and asked me what I was doing for Thanksgiving. I told her that I had planned to go back to Los Angeles, and she said, "If you change your mind, I'd like to make Thanksgiving dinner for you." I actually thought about it because Phyllis, my wife, and I were having some sort of disagreement or problem. However, I thought better of it when push came to shove at the end of our tour.

While we were in Columbus, a flu was going around. Al Jardine insisted that we all get Asian Flu shots. I came down with a bad case in Boston, making dinner with Maureen in Columbus altogether impossible even if I had decided to return. Besides, my family was gathering at my cousin's home for Thanksgiving dinner. I got there, apparently to the surprise of everyone, sick as a dog, tried to be wonderful and not complain, but finally staggered home for a stay in bed.

WE DO NATIONAL TELEVISION

On one of our trips, we started in New York City, not for a concert gig, but for an appearance on *The Ed Sullivan Show*. We flew into town a day or two early for meetings with the Ed Sullivan staff. I had a long discussion with the production people about the two songs they were to perform. The Beach Boys had their own ideas, but the show staff wanted two others. I know Carl wanted to do two of their new songs. I told him I'd ask, but that he shouldn't hold out much hope. In the long run, the Ed Sullivan people won out.

That night, Nick wanted everyone to experience one of New York's famous restaurants. Since The Beach Boys were paying for it, we ended up at 21, which was about as famous as it gets in New York. Nick called for a wine list and handed it to me.

"You're the wine expert," he said. "You pick it. Needless to say, they had an extensive list of fine wines, and again, as long as I wasn't paying for it, I was going to order the best. The book must have had more than a hundred pages of labels.

Pointing to a fine year of *La Romanee*, I asked for that. They were out. I asked for another year, but they were out of that. Continuing to show off, I tried *La Tache*. They didn't have any in stock. I asked for a *Chateau Lafite*, then a *Latour*, an *Haut Brion* and finally a *Margaux*. I was showing off my really limited knowledge and I can talk a good game, but they were out of them all. In desperation, I asked for a German white wine, which they did have.

The following morning, we all gathered at the Ed Sullivan Theater for an eight o'clock music rehearsal. The engineering people worked out some special visual effects including the use of vertical mirrors for one song. That was going to be good. In fact, their set design and construction people were wonderful and gave The Beach Boys as good a setting as was possible on a variety show.

After blocking for the cameras, I went to the control booth to discuss the way we would like the music mixed. I was told to come back after lunch.

DAMON RUNYON HAD NOTHING ON US, ONLY HE CALLED IT "MINDY'S"

I had heard of Lindy's and it's famous, sarcastic waiters, all of whom had been there twenty-five years or more. It was due to close its doors forever, and since it was more than likely my last chance, I wanted to experience it. Lindy's, together with the Stage and the Carnegie, were probably the most famous delicatessens in the country, if not the world. I had already done the Stage and the Carnegie on my visit to set the Maharishi tour. I had eaten in Miami Beach at Wolfie's, Pumpernicks, and the Famous, but had never gotten to Lindy's, and I sure wasn't going to pass up the opportunity.

The Beach Boys wanted to go along, and naturally, so did Nick. The waiters lived up to their surly reputation, but in a way I can only describe as friendly way. I ordered blintzes, and when we finished, our waiter returned for desert orders.

My absolute favorite pie is Dutch Apple, and since it was on the menu, I ordered it. The waiter said, "Try the pineapple cheesecake. It's very good." There, the waiters were never wrong and the customers were never right, unless you were someone they knew very well.

"No thanks," I said, "I really want the pie."

"Try the cheesecake, we're famous for it."

"Thanks, really, but honestly, I love Dutch Apple pie."

"I'm telling you, do yourself a favor, have the cheesecake. I promise you, you'll double my tip."

"No, really."

"Listen," he said, "you're obviously not from around here. This will probably be your last chance to try our famous pineapple cheesecake. Who knows if we'll ever make it again after today."

"Honestly," I said, "I'm sure you are right about your cheesecake, but I'm practically compulsive about Dutch Apple. Not every restaurant has it, you know."

"I will admit," he said, "that our Dutch Apple pie is exceptionally good. You could take a piece home with you. But you shouldn't miss the pineapple cheesecake."

In my opinion, New York cheesecake had the consistency and taste of library paste. We went back and forth a few more times, and he said finally, "Okay, you don't know what you're missing, but Dutch Apple it is."

He brought me pineapple cheesecake. No joke.

WE ALMOST SCREW UP ED SULLIVAN

Back at the theater, the production staff had set the stage the way it would be that night for the live show so the group could walk through the act. We were informed that The Beach Boys would have to lip sync and pretend to play their instruments. They insisted that was the way it was done on *The Ed Sullivan*

Show. The Beach Boys were adamant that they would only do their songs live.

The engineer said, "Everyone lip syncs."

We argued, "Everyone *else* lip syncs because they're incapable of sounding like their records when they do it live. The Beach Boys *never* lip sync."

The argument ended in a tie. They could sing live, but the music would have to be on a track so the engineers could control the volume. In order for us to do that, we had to wait until everyone else had rehearsed and the Sullivan band left for the night.

The band finished around five o'clock, and sometime around nine or nine-thirty, we finally got a track that Carl thought was good enough. Because there would be no time to bring in Dennis's drums for the taping of the track, he used the drums from the house band for the music track. Dennis was extremely strong. He was so strong that we carried at least a half-dozen extra snare and bass drum skins because he was always breaking them. We even carried extra bass drum pedals, because he broke *them*, too, which drummers rarely did.

AL AND I TEST THE NIGHTLIFE

That night, Al Jardine and I, having nothing better to do, opted for a late supper and some girl ogling at the Brasserie, a place well-known for girls worth ogling. We ran into our sound man, Steve Desper, with Bruce Johnston, who had a date with an old, only in the sense that he knew her for some time, flame. We hung together until Bruce and his date left for some private time, and Steve went elsewhere.

Al and I managed to converse with some young ladies who recognized him, but obviously weren't impressed. Neither Al nor I had whatever they were looking for that night, so they went on their way. Not that we were interested in anything beyond ogling.

We did meet a young girl who seemed very friendly towards both of us, so while she was away from the booth for a moment, we tossed a coin to see who would walk her back to her apartment and whatever might follow. As I said, she was very friendly and prospects seemed high. I won the coin toss, which upset Alan because, after all, *he* was a Beach Boy! We walked perhaps five or six blocks to a huge apartment complex, complete with guard and security system. She took me up to her one-bedroom apartment, which it turned out she shared with four other girls, all of whom were home when we got there. As I have previously mentioned, life was like that.

The next evening, we returned to the theater to wait our turn in the Green Room when I heard the band drummer yelling, "Who the fuck ruined my drum? I've been using this same skin for five years and some sonofabitch stretched it."

We could hardly deny that the stretching was done by Dennis, so I offered to pay for a new one. I would have replaced it from Dennis's supply if the equipment truck hadn't been in another city already. He did accept the offer of payment and was somehow able to find a replacement before show time.

Before The Beach Boys went on, we did our best to tell the sound man what balance we wanted, but he refused to listen, preferring to do it in whatever manner he deemed proper, which in that case, was somewhat louder than they were singing. He obviously didn't like rock and roll or thought that all rock acts just played loud and sang lousy. As far as we were concerned, he screwed up what could have been wonderful exposure and a good performance. His attitude seemed to be, "I know what's good and what's bad and screw you and the horse you rode in on."

While we were in New York, we took advantage of our free time at night to visit the Bitter End, a comedy club in Greenwich Village, and to eat at the Tin Angel, a delightful little restaurant that was above the Dugout, a small restaurant and bar right next door to the Bitter End. It was at the Tin Angel where we discovered a drink called Plum Soup. Of course, it wasn't soup at all, but an alcoholic beverage, which we consumed as though they were like soup.

Sunday until show time was pretty much an off day. I had lunch at Max Asnas' Stage Deli, and spent the rest of the time at the hotel, working. Following the performance, a group of us returned to the Tin Angel for more plum soup.

We had trouble trying to find the airport at night in New Jersey. I had broken my glasses leaving Columbus, Ohio, and I had to rely on Carl to read the road signs as he was sitting in the front seat directing us to the airport, which was probably in Elizabeth. It was snowing, and the access road to which we had been directed was under repair. We had to follow barely visible detour signs as best we could, signs I couldn't read without my distance glasses, and to which Carl paid little attention. Fortunately, we had given ourselves lots of leeway and found our way to the airport just in time for our flight to Boston.

I PROVE THAT IRVING WASN'T ALWAYS RIGHT

There we were in Boston. Sales had indeed gone well, just as Fred Taylor predicted. We were doing two shows at the Music Hall Theater, a movie palace that once housed legitimate shows and vaudeville. As I mentioned a little earlier, I didn't have a lot of money from Nick for promotion and so tried something that no one had ever done in Boston before as far as I knew. Fred Taylor thought it was worth a try.

I decided not to spend a nickel on metropolitan newspaper advertising, contrary to everything Irving ever taught me. He always invested heavily in good-sized ads. I spent a good portion of my meager budget on college and even high school newspapers, which were very cheap, and some of it to have a two-minute film made promoting The Beach Boys and the date.

The Music Hall Theater played the promotional film at every intermission for two weeks prior to the concert and that certainly helped.

THE RETURN OF PRISCILLA OF BANGOR

I was in my hotel room getting cleaned up and changing clothes before leaving for the theater, when the telephone rang. It was not, as I thought it might be, a call from Carl or Mike, but from Priscilla, the girl I met in Bangor and for whom I left a pair of tickets.

She had already picked up one of the tickets—I guess she worked alone—and wanted to know whether I could arrange for her to meet The Beach Boys afterwards. In fact, what she really wanted was to have sex with them all if she could. She especially wanted to have Bruce and Dennis, "because they were the sexiest," but if possible, every one of them, and maybe some select members of the supporting act.

I don't recall anyone objecting, but I can't honestly say who took Priscilla up on her offer. When we got back to the hotel, I called Bruce and told him there was a young woman in my room, very anxious to meet him. He said, "Send her over," and I went across the street to a delicatessen because I hadn't eaten at all that day.

Eventually, I returned to my room and read for about two hours when the telephone rang. It was Priscilla. I thought she might have run out of Beach Boys and that I was next on her list. However, it was not to be. It seemed that someone from hotel security spotted her wandering around the halls and was trying to throw her out. She wanted to hide out in my room until the heat died down and she could contact the rest of her list. You had to admire the girl's stamina. I had no objection to her request, and a few minutes later, she showed up, having successfully avoided detection.

By then, she had the room numbers of everyone she wanted to see. My name wasn't on the list, but to tell the truth, the idea of being about tenth on her screw agenda was not really appealing, even if *she* was. She waited about ten minutes, called the next name in line and disappeared for the night. I never heard from her again, but I never did another show in Boston, either.

THE BEGINNING OF THE END

The "problem" I mentioned about that Boston date once again involved Nick. Fred Taylor showed up at the theater with all his bills in hand. After settling the box office with Fred's help, I turned a lot of money over to Nick from which I presumed he was going to reimburse Fred.

Nick took the bills and said, in essence, "Gee, Fred, I'd give you a check for this, but I left the company check book back in Los Angeles. I'll send you the money just as soon as I get home." I took Nick at his word and didn't think about it again.

It wasn't until several weeks later that I heard from Fred, who informed me that Nick hadn't yet repaid him, or even paid his $500 fee, a minuscule amount only because of our friendship. The fact that Nick had reneged on a debt was one of the prime reasons I left; another being that I was having difficulty in getting money from him to produce any more concerts. I learned later that Fred finally had to sue The Beach Boys to get his money.

CHAPTER EIGHTEEN:
A Hodge Podge of Stuff

Before my problem with Boston and Fred Taylor, American Productions was running smoothly, whenever Nick would free up enough money to produce some concerts on our own. Margaret, our gorgeous secretary, handled her job well, and most everyone in the office was having a good time, except Nick, of course, who was totally paranoid over the friendships Dick and I had with the girls in the office. He had a right to be paranoid, I suppose, because the girls who worked for him talked to us freely about what was actually going on in the company.

Around that time, Dennis Wilson developed a friendship with the infamous Charles Manson, whose entourage, at Manson's urging, killed a number of Hollywood personalities. However, long before that, Dennis moved them all into his Pacific Palisades ranch home. The primary reason for the friendship, as far as I could see, was that Charley had something like seventeen girls following him around who would provide any kind of sex Dennis wanted, whenever he wanted it.

Dennis and Charley started writing songs together and in fact did write one song Dennis wanted to include on the *20/20* album. Dennis also wanted Charley's name to appear in the credits and to receive royalties, something to which none of us would agree. Eventually, a check to Charley resolved the matter.

Almost every time Dennis came to the office, he had Charley in tow, and often three or four of Charley's "Angels." While Dennis took care of whatever business he had, usually demanding and getting more money from Nick, Charley sat in the hallway near the top of the stairs, which meant that any visitor had to pass him or step over him to get back to our offices.

There were really two reasons we wanted Charley out of there: First, he blocked the hallway, and second, he was generally shoeless and unwashed. We decided to move him to where he would be out of the way and out of sight.

I said, "Charley, why don't you just go sit in the corner of my office and wait for Dennis?"

That was fine with Charley; he didn't care where he sat. He found a place in the corner of my office behind my desk and just sat there quietly strumming his guitar, until Dennis was ready to leave.

Nick apparently discovered that Charley was wanted on some charge in San Francisco and notified the police. They came and picked him up, and Charley disappeared for a few months. He eventually returned and moved back into Dennis's ranch home. Before long, and to our general relief, he moved on to the ranch in the San Fernando Valley from which he increased his drug operations and ordered the murders for which he is still in prison.

Of all The Beach Boys, Dennis and I were closest because I never treated him like a child. He frequently invited me to his ranch so I could utilize the services of Charles Manson's girls, and just as frequently, I found reasons to turn him down. He really thought he was doing me a favor.

He said, "They'll do anything I tell them to and they'll do the same for you." Obviously, I refused the offer. I wasn't crazy. I told him, "Dennis, I don't need to get laid that bad. I wouldn't do it with *your* dick."

A RETURN TO THE "BILLBOARD TOP 100"

About that time, everyone from Capitol Records was pushing The Beach Boys to write some new material and record a new album because it had been about two years since the last one, which had not sold particularly well, even though it was a good album, but just different. At that time, Dennis was living below a friend's residence in one of the canyons and he wanted a piano there so he could write without having to come into the office every day. Nick rented a piano for him and had it delivered.

A few weeks later, Dennis came in and asked everyone to listen to a song he had just finished and of which he was obviously very proud. We, girls included, followed him into the music room, where he pecked out his new tune on the piano. Nick gushed that it was wonderful; that Dennis should go right to the studio and record it. Dick and I said it was terrible.

We took Dennis aside and said, "Dennis, what you guys really need is something familiar; something in your old style." Their recent single releases had been less than successful, although stalwart fans of The Beach Boys did buy to some extent. Personally, I thought some of the songs were very good, but they were different, too "far out" for most of their fans. Either the public didn't understand or wouldn't accept that "new" music. We suggested he go home and try again.

Our suggestion wasn't particularly brilliant; it was simply obvious. The result was "Do It Again," which became a big hit.

When the song was recorded, Dick hired a cinematographer to shoot a three-minute film to go with the record. It may have been the precursor of music videos. We took Brian, Dennis, Carl, Alan, and Bruce to a park in the Pacific Palisades, where they played on swings and ran around to the cameraman's direction.

I brought along a bat, some gloves, and a couple of softballs. When Brian saw them, he got very excited. Even though he was pretty much non compos mentis much of the time, considering his problems with drugs and with his marriage, he straightened up instantly at the sight of the softball equipment and began hitting balls for the rest of us to shag.

When the cinematographer finished in the park, everyone except me—I went back to the office—headed down to the ocean for some surfing shots. Bruce, it seemed, was the only current surfer in the group. Even though Dennis was the group's original surfer, and as the pop music world knows, suggested to Brian that he write a song about surfing, Dennis did only some body surfing on a rubber raft for the film. They used the talents of a young man named Corky Corcoran (or something akin to that) for the actual surfing footage.

ROCK AND ROLL GOES HISTORIC

The fact that Brian had become a recluse has been well-documented, but there were times when he was lucid, or reasonably so. Sometime in 1968 or early 1969, I received a telephone call from writer Pete Johnson, then a working for KHJ radio. They wanted to present the history of rock and roll over a series of broadcasts on their station, something that has since been copied dozens, perhaps hundreds of times by other rock stations. I thought it was a great idea.

"I have to interview Brian," he said.

"Yeah, I agree, but I don't know if he's capable of being interviewed."

"It wouldn't be complete if we didn't have Brian, because everyone knows he's the number one genius of rock."

Again I agreed with him, but didn't know what I could do about it. I promised to get back to him once I talked to Brian. I didn't even know if I could reach him, because Brian frequently wouldn't take telephone calls. Generally, we had to go through his wife, Marilyn, or one of the brothers, but I tried, and amazingly, was able to speak with him directly.

As I suspected, Brian didn't want to do it. It was senseless to argue at that point, because he didn't actually have a reason for not being interviewed, but logic and common sense were not then Brian's strong points. Then, I got an idea and called Pete.

"Listen, Pete," I said, "how about letting me do the interview? I'll be careful to leave space between Brian's answers and my questions so you can just cut me out and insert your voice." He agreed that it would work, and I called Brian again.

He still wasn't sure, but that time agreed to come into the office late some afternoon so we could try it without interruption and without any pressure. I told him, "Look, if it doesn't work, or you don't like it, we'll just dump it." A week or so later, we sat down in my office and casually talked about all sorts of things, about how he was feeling; how Marilyn was feeling; what, if anything, he was writing; everything I could think of including the kind of questions I was going to ask. I pretty much planned to wing the actual taped interview if we were going to do it.

"I don't know," Brian hesitated. "I'm not sure I can do this."

"Sure you can," I said. "Why don't we give it a try?"

Within a few minutes, he loosened up and got into the spirit of the interview and was clearly enjoying himself. We used up two hours of audio tape by the time I figured we had covered enough, and besides, I was running out of questions.

"That was fun," he said. "Let's do it again. I think I can do it better." He wanted to listen to the entire tape, but I talked him into settling for a few minutes because it was getting late and I wanted to get home. It wasn't that he was disappointed with the first tape, but he flat out enjoyed doing it. I think it had a lot to do with the fact that it was just one-on-one conversation with no pressure. It may have been the longest talk he and I ever had.

I took the first tape out of the recorder and put it aside because I had no idea what this second effort might produce.

"I'm not sure I can remember what I asked you," I said.

He said, "That's okay, let's just do it."

So we did. I sent both tapes to Pete, who did remove my voice and the history of rock and roll made it to radio.

WE ALL LEARN MORE ABOUT NICK

One very hot day, I guess the air conditioning wasn't working or not performing up to snuff, so Margaret, our secretary, removed her bra and put it in her desk drawer. Margaret was very well-endowed and it was readily apparent that she was bra-less, although she could get away with it because she was really beautifully constructed. Neither Dick nor I made anything of it and nothing was said until she packed up to go home that night and she discovered her brassiere was missing. She accused Dick and me of hiding it; said she didn't think it was very funny, and that she wanted it back, and right now. We denied having any knowledge of its whereabouts.

We found it the next day, when Nick left the office on some business. Lynette, his secretary, opened the door with her remote and there it was in Nick's middle desk drawer.

In the end, I did my best to tell The Beach Boys about Nick, but they didn't believe me . . . not for another year or so. I ran into Carl at Studio Instrument Rentals where they were rehearsing.

He said, "We fired Nick. Sometimes it takes me awhile to accept things, but when I do, it doesn't take me long to do something about it. You were right about him."

BACK TO THEIR ROOTS

I mentioned earlier that The Beach Boys did not receive the recognition they deserved in Los Angeles, but they were heroes at Hawthorne High, where at least Brian and Dennis went to school. Carl, for a time, was a student at Hollywood Professional High School. A call from a student at Hawthorne was routed to me concerning the availability of The Beach Boys for a dance. The young man, a member of his prom committee, wanted to know if The Beach Boys would consider playing for their senior prom, which was going to be held in the ballroom at the Beverly Hilton hotel.

The date was open, but it seemed a little ludicrous. I asked how much money they had to spend, knowing it wouldn't be very much. It wasn't. They had $900. I suggested that he shouldn't hold out too much hope, but that I would take the offer to them.

I talked it over with Dick and he also thought it would be fun and might help their image in Los Angeles. All we had to do was talk The Beach Boys into it. Surprisingly, it didn't take much convincing at all. They thought it would be great fun and gave the okay to approve the date. At that time, The Beach Boys were working with a blues and soul singer named Joe Hicks, and they added him to the show at no cost to the school.

We were all decked out in tuxedos for the evening. The Beach Boys played a full dance set; Joe Hicks sang, and the kids loved the show and dance. Dick and I got to relive and compare notes about our own proms, but weren't allowed to go out and dance—or even talk—with any of the young people. Everyone, even the Wilson brothers, who were students at Hawthorne, were barred from anywhere but back stage.

I guess the teacher/chaperons thought our presence would somehow contaminate the youngsters. It was okay for The Beach Boys to donate a $20,000 night, but not to mingle with teenagers, even though Dennis and Carl were barely out of their teens themselves. I suppose Dick and I qualified as "dirty old men" in their minds and everyone else as "dirty *young* men."

Incidentally, Dennis managed to lose the piano we rented for him. I asked him, "How the hell can you lose a piano?" He said he loaned it to someone and couldn't remember who.

"How do you lend someone a piano?" I asked. "You can hardly drive over and pick it up in a car, even a big one."

Dennis just couldn't recall and we ended up paying for it.

CHAPTER NINETEEN:
We Do the
Responsible Thing

I was spending more time on the road since I then had two hats to wear, although Dick did go back on the road for a trip through Canada, the trip to Europe, and finally, all the time after I quit in April 1969. The Canadian trip was one I couldn't have possibly done alone since part of it would have required me to be in two countries at one time. Some of the shows were in the United States, while I was busy advancing dates in Canada and dealing with the Canadian government.

We started one series of dates in Norman at the University of Oklahoma. Mike Love had flown off to Rishikesh, India, to personally deliver $5,000 to the Maharishi, promising to meet us in time for the first performance. He didn't make it.

We arrived at the University field house as the portable seats were still being set up on the basketball floor. Several cheerleader types gathered around the stage and in the bleachers, as Carl led the rehearsal. I said, "Don't do everything or these people won't need to pay to see the show." Steve Desper, our sound man, also needed to test the acoustics of the vast hall, where basketball was the primary attraction. Since they hadn't been on the road for some time, and didn't get together at all when they weren't touring except to discuss material, they really needed to rehearse.

There was also the problem of what to do if Mike Love didn't return to Oklahoma in time for the show. Billy Hinsche, Carl's brother-in-law, and one third of Dino, Desi, and Billy, was traveling with us, I guess to keep Carl company, or because Carl wanted to give him some work. We planned to use him strictly as an extra guitarist.

As the hour for the show grew closer, we still hadn't heard from Mike. I went to Billy and asked, "Can you sing Mike's part?" When you realize that Mike was the lead singer on almost every song, it was quite a burden. We had a quick conference and some other songs were split among Carl and Bruce.

Billy was willing to give it a shot, although he couldn't play the Theremin, the sound device so important to "Good Vibrations." As it happened, he couldn't even recall all the lyrics to the songs he did sing, but apparently the Oklahoma students either didn't notice or didn't care.

Thinking back, I remember once asking Herb Jeffries, a famous singer of the 1940s, why he didn't sing the right words to some songs, and he replied, "Why should I bother? They don't know the words anyway." I guess he was right.

I had one serious disagreement with Carl about his music selections before that tour. Carl wanted to do mostly new songs that were largely from the *Wild Honey* and *Friends* albums. We argued that people came to hear the older, more familiar music, but Carl was adamant.

We felt that in the past, when they did new material, the audience seemed to lose interest, particularly when they did it on the second half of the show. Carl finally agreed that they would open with new songs and then after intermission, close with the songs that made them famous.

Back at the hotel, there was a message from Margaret, my secretary, confirming that Mike had been snowed in and was stranded in India. He sent word that he would definitely join us at the next date in Omaha, Nebraska, and so Billy became Mike for just one night.

The concert went well enough, and Herb Jeffries was right that no one noticed that Billy didn't know all the lyrics. After we informed the audience that Mike was snowed in on a mountain top somewhere, they took it well. I guess it was something akin to what happened when Brian Wilson quit the road. He was replaced by Glen Campbell, who had already played on several of their studio sessions. I wonder, looking back, how many people even noticed that it wasn't Brian. After all, Glen was tall and he wore their red and white-striped shirt.

Shortly after we checked into the hotel in Omaha, our next stop, I got a call from a girl waiting in the lobby. She needed to see me. She identified herself as a Linda, friend of Mike's, so naturally, I went down to the lobby.

She approached me and asked, "Are you Jack Lloyd?"

She said that she was Mike Love's girlfriend, not just a friend. They met on a previous visit and she seemed to think they had a more than special relationship. When she discovered Mike hadn't checked in, she naturally asked for Dick Duryea, and when she learned he wasn't with the group either, she got my name from someone. She asked if she could hang out with me to wait for Mike.

I didn't want to disillusion her by telling her that he not only had a wife and kids, but that he had "special" girlfriends everywhere. Linda told me she had spoken with Mike a few weeks earlier about having some of The Beach Boys visit the Shriner's Childrens' Hospital the morning of our concert. I saw no reason why they shouldn't do it, but explained that Mike had failed to communicate the information to me or anyone else.

Fortunately, she and I ran into Bruce Johnston and Alan Jardine in the lobby and they agreed to go. Carl, Billy, and Dennis didn't want to get up that early and begged off. Of course, Mike wasn't there, so there was nothing we could do about that unless he happened to show up late that night or very early the next morning. Linda said she would have a couple of cars at the hotel around nine the next morning to pick us up.

I got up early and went down to the Lobby around eight thirty. Linda was already waiting. Bruce and Alan arrived a few moments later, just as Carl, Dennis, and Billy were coming out of the restaurant. I told them that as long as they were up, they had to join us at the hospital. They groused a little, but finally agreed to go along.

Arriving at the hospital, we were met by a nurse, who ushered us into a large room full of young people seated in a semi-circle. Some were in wheel chairs, some were propped up in hospital beds that had been wheeled in, and some were on crutches. Another nurse approached me and said, "We're all so excited that your people are going to play for the children." Another surprise.

I had no idea what to say to her because Linda hadn't mentioned anything about a performance. That created a rather large problem since no one bothered to bring instruments; we hadn't even thought about it. I turned to the boys and asked them what they wanted to do. There was an old upright piano in the room, and Bruce said he would play that and maybe they could do a couple of numbers. Carl, looking around the room at the children, was practically in tears. He turned to me and said, "See if they can find a box guitar around somewhere." Dennis added, "Maybe they've got something I can use for drumsticks."

They managed to locate an old acoustic guitar that probably hadn't been tuned in years, but no drum sticks. In the meantime, Dennis had located an empty plastic trash can that he turned over for use as a drum, and decided he could keep the beat with his hands.

In that way, The Beach Boys played their first "charity" concert. They liked it so much that after I resigned, they had Dick set up other events, even playing for prisoners at McAlister State Prison in Oklahoma.

After the "show," we toured all the wards, stopping at every bed where communication was even remotely possible. It was a gut-wrenching experience. None of us had ever seen a hydrocephalic child, or children born without limbs, including one youngster, who had been born without arms or legs and was propped up in a wheel chair. At the bottom floor, just adjacent to the stairs, we found a small chapel.

Carl said, "I think it would be a good idea for all of us to go in there and meditate for awhile." Everyone agreed.

On the drive back to the hotel, Linda again asked if she could hang out with me while she waited for Mike, and that was certainly okay with me. She was very pretty with long hair, and as mentioned before, Mike was very fond of girls with long hair. During the course of the day, we got to know one another reasonably well, and about an hour before the concert, she asked, "If Mike doesn't get here, can I spend the night with you?"

Well, no one had ever offered me anything like that before, so I said, "Sure, but I assure you, Mike will make this date." He did. Five minutes before curtain.

MIKE HAS A ROUTINE FOR TRAVEL

Back in Los Angeles, when we were making hotel reservations for the tour, Mike stopped in my office to ask that we not make any room reservations for him. I asked what he planned to do about sleeping arrangements, and he replied, "Don't worry. If I ever need a room, we'll get one then."

He had developed an opening for the show by conversing with the audience before they started playing. Since he was deeply involved in Transcendental Meditation, he asked if there were any TM people out there. There always were, and he invited them all back stage after the concert. From that group, he selected a few promising young women, and if anyone lived alone, he got himself invited to her place for the night. In Omaha, Mike needed a room since Linda apparently didn't live alone.

The tour included a stop in Springfield at the Illinois State Fair. At the same time, The Beatles were appearing in Chicago. Mike Love and Bruce Johnston got one or more of The Beatles on the telephone, and after a long conversation, decided they were going to fly to Chicago right after our show, visit with their friends, and then join us at the next date.

Dennis didn't want to go, and Jon Parks, Steve Korthoff, and I ended up in Dennis's room just shooting the breeze. Dennis decided he was hungry and Dennis insisted that we call for room service to send someone over with a menu. There was no sense arguing with him. A young man showed up within a few minutes and we ordered. Dennis decided he wanted a whole pie for himself, which we thought was pretty selfish. I think the rest of us ordered iced tea and maybe some sort of ready-to-eat nosh. Dennis said to the waiter, "If you get back in nine minutes, I'll give you a $9 tip."

Eight and a half minutes later, the young man was standing at the door, with the pie in one hand, the nosh stuffed into his pockets, and three glasses of iced tea—one in each hand and one in the front pocket of his jacket. I insisted that Dennis give him $9.

Dennis said, "You give it to him and I'll give it back to you."

I said, "No, you've got the money, so you pay him. I know you . . . if I give it to him, I'll never see it, so I want *you* to pay it."

Mike, Bruce, and Carl were in Chicago around the time that The Beach Boys released "Good Vibrations." Brian got a call from George Harrison, John Lennon, and Paul McCartney, who told him, "You've shown us the way." The result of being "shown the way" was the *Sergeant Pepper* album, a whole new attack for The Beatles.

I may be prejudiced, but I have always considered The Beach Boys as much an influence on the music of the 1960s as The Beatles. The Beatles certainly thought so. I remember when *New Musical Express*, an English music publication, took a poll to determine the most popular group in the world. The winner was not The Beatles, as one might expect, but The Beach Boys. That is not to denigrate The Beatles, who also changed the course of rock music, but The Beach Boys had done the same thing before them.

CHAPTER TWENTY:
Better Than First Class

We made several trips in John Mecom's four-engine Viscount, a propeller-driven airplane that came fully equipped with booze, nosh, and a steward named John. Mr. Mecom was the owner of the New Orleans Saints of the National Football League, and he had himself a very nicely appointed airplane.

On those trips, Dick and I were traveling together. We were on the road for close to three weeks, and I had all my clothes in one fold-over bag and a smaller carry-on bag. The fold-over bag was so heavy that no one wanted or could handle it alone, not even Dennis, who was stronger than anyone else. Since we were flying charter, there were no baggage handlers other than ourselves, and the luggage had to be stored on two bunks in the forward section of the airplane. We needed the cargo hold for equipment. That meant every bag had to be handed up the stairs and into the airplane, like an old-fashioned bucket brigade at a fire.

I was drinking Jack Daniels in those days, although I would generally settle for V.O. or Canadian Club. Dick, being a Scotch drinker, was imbibing Cutty Sark. However, Mr. Mecom wasn't stocking Jack Daniels, V.O., or Canadian Club, so I settled for Wild Turkey. We frequently went right from a hall to an airport, so one of the nicest things about having a steward was that when we arrived at the airplane after a concert, John was waiting at the top of the steps with a triple Wild Turkey for me and a triple Cutty Sark for Dick.

Also, John made sure there were things like dry-roasted peanuts and junk food available for everyone. Part of his job was to arrange for sandwiches and occasionally hot food when we traveled at night, so no one ever went hungry.

That airplane was equipped with leather easy chairs that swiveled, a stereo and tape deck, tables, and couches. It was luxurious, particularly for the time. Mike liked charter traveling so much that he had me check into the cost of a used Lear or similar jet; something that would accommodate ten people. The more than $1 million price tag killed any more thoughts of owning their own airplane, although there was some thought given to buying a DC-3 when Trans Texas Airlines switched to DC-9 jets. You could buy a DC-3 for $25,000. The cost of converting it to a luxury airship would have been another $10,000, and extra engines were $5,000 each.

It was on one of the trips in the Viscount that Dennis got bored and wanted to play Gin Rummy with me for money. Irving Granz warned me against playing with Dennis because when he lost—and he usually did—he never paid up. I told Dennis the only card game I played was Cribbage, and since he didn't know the game, we couldn't play cards at all. He demanded that I teach him the game, and to his credit, he was an amazingly fast study.

Cribbage is not a difficult game to play once you learn the basics about what combinations score points and how many points they score. Dennis caught on to that part of the game quickly, but he could never think ahead or finesse something out of a bad hand. He loved playing so much that he began carrying a deck of cards with him to get me into a game whenever I wasn't busy, when we were in the air, or whenever he felt like it—such as at three o'clock in the morning.

I told Dennis that I would teach him the game the same way I learned it—for money; not a lot, to be sure, but only if there was something on the line would he learn the finer points of the game. Of course, he never beat me, and of course, he never paid me, either. Dennis had such an endearing quality in those days that I never got mad at him, except that one time when we played at Virginia Polytechnic Institute in Blacksburg and he snorted some cocaine before the show.

Dennis ended up so hooked on Cribbage that he often knocked on my door in the middle of the night, usually after his date took care of his sexual needs, or if he threw her out because she didn't. It didn't matter what time it was. He'd be there, shouting something like, "I've got a deck of cards, let's play Cribbage."

I'd yell back from bed, "Go away, I want to sleep!" but he'd just stand there pounding away until I got up and let him in.

THE BEACH BOYS CONQUER THE COUNTRY TO THE NORTH

We used the Viscount for our big Canadian tour. A Canadian promoter had purchased four dates, Winnipeg, Edmonton, Regina, and Vancouver, through our booking agency. With those dates as a base, we decided to add four more Canadian cities and promote them ourselves. The agency sold a couple of additional concerts in the United States to fill out the tour.

Our contract with the Canadian promoter called for deposits of something like $7,500, but the money wasn't forthcoming by the deadline, which was worrisome in view of the work we had already done, the money we fronted for our own four dates, and our need for capital. The agency contacted him, and then they assured us that the deposits were on their way and we should go straight ahead with our plans, which we did.

Dick and I selected St. John, New Brunswick, Halifax, Nova Scotia, Montreal, Quebec, and the capitol city, Ottawa, Ontario, and I immediately began the promotional work.

After setting deals with ticket sellers, radio stations, newspapers, and a couple of local promoters that knew the areas better than we, I went out to make a promotional swing through all eight cities, spending time with box office personnel primarily in the four cities we sold, plus everyone connected with our own dates.

Over the previous two and a half years, I had gotten friendly over the telephone with many of the people in Canadian box offices because Irving Granz produced concerts there. I had sold souvenir book in Vancouver and Victoria, but Irving always did the eastern part of Canada.

By the time I made my first trip, radio and newspaper advertising for all eight dates had started and early ticket sales looked promising. Dick, who was apparently back in favor, handled the United States trips, which was fortunate in light of the fact that I had to briefly leave the group for my confrontations with the Canadian government while they were working in the United States. As I toured each of the cities our booking agency sold to the Canadian promoter, I discovered that he had been raiding box office receipts from very early on in order to pay his bills. I asked each box office to stop giving him money, explaining that we hadn't received our deposits yet. Unfortunately, without his consent, there was no way I could get my hands on box office money to cover the deposits he still owed us.

They all agreed not to give him access to any more funds, which engendered the first call back from him. Dick told him there was no way we'd let him take any more money, even though he was paying the box offices, until we got our deposits. He finally gave up trying because it was obvious there was no way we were going to change our minds, unless, of course, we saw some cashier's checks first—and not out of box office funds.

He promised to send checks immediately, and Dick said, "Just as soon as we cash them, we'll release the box offices." The checks never arrived.

Dick tried tracing him down through the telephone numbers he gave us, because we really needed the cash. He discovered one number was actually a pay telephone in a liquor store. However, some of the box office people had prior relations with him, which was why they let him draw on ticket sales in the first place, and they felt pretty sure we would eventually get our money. Still, we had a lot of company money invested in the tour and we didn't want to lose it.

On that first promotional trip around Canada, I flew directly to Montreal, since that was as far eastward as I could go on a direct flight. Air Canada then featured their *Galaxy* flight to Montreal, and it was their "showcase" flight. As usual, I flew first class, which meant I got to wait for the flight in the first class lounge, where I discovered to my delight, they served Crown Royal, a Canadian blended whiskey, for free.

Not long after we were airborne, I wandered forward to the lounge, where seats were set facing one another with tables between them. There was a wet bar with a real, live bartender, who made sure my glass of Crown Royal and water was never empty. As I was the only passenger taking advantage of that section of the airplane, I was his only steady customer.

In a rack at every table was a deck of cards and a cribbage board. One of the stewardesses (they didn't call them Flight Attendants yet) came by to talk. I asked if she played and if she would like to join me in a game. She did, and we played for about an hour, until it was time to serve dinner.

Dinner was remarkable for an airplane, but good for *any* restaurant. The usual main course was a roast that was actually cooked, not merely reheated, on the airplane. The bartender was also the chef, and he often had to leave me and my glass to go below to the galley.

With each course, they served a different but excellent French or German wine; none of the typical domestic crap. I remember a whole cold glazed trout as an appetizer, with a white German wine, and then some sort of hot appetizer, possibly veal or lamb, with a hearty Bordeaux. The stewardess delivered a sorbet between each course to clear the palate. Then, the roast, which was carved at our seat, was followed by five or six kinds of desert, and of course, more wine. Finally, we were served a choice of after-dinner liqueurs, brandies, cheeses, and fruit.

After dinner, we played a little more cribbage, and I felt the airplane beginning to descend. I knew there was a stop in Toronto, but when the stewardess came by to explain that all passengers had to deplane here, I said, "I can't get off the airplane, I can't even stand up."

She added, "Sorry, Jack, you not only have to get off and go through customs, you have to collect and carry your own bags."

I AVOID WHAT COULD HAVE BEEN AN INTERNATIONAL INCIDENT

I didn't know about having to go through customs at our first stop in a country because I never had to do that driving into Mexico, and up to that point in my life, I had never been to any other foreign country, other than that one trip to Vancouver, which was the first stop.

My luggage consisted, as usual, of my giant garment bag, a shoulder bag, and my attaché case. I was busy regretting the garment bag as I dragged it along the floor to the customs officer. Among the items in the attaché case were a couple dozen photographs of The Beach

Boys, probably eight or ten of their latest record albums to distribute to radio stations, and my "starter" pistol in a fancy leather holster I purchased in North Miami Beach to make the "gun" look more realistic.

Although it happened in the past to Irving when he went to Canada, I had completely forgotten that the Canadian authorities frequently collected import duties on things they thought could be sold, like records and photographs, and thus generate income for themselves.

I remembered it just as I was nearing the customs desk. My problem, other than being slightly tipsy, was that while I had *some* money with me, it was barely enough to cover my expenses for the week, let alone any possible import duties. I was pretty sure customs wouldn't take a credit card, and besides, I didn't want to use it unless absolutely necessary because Nick wasn't always good about reimbursing us.

Somehow, I managed to drag my entire luggage to the counter, where a lone customs inspector stood. I remember thinking, *This isn't much of a customs office*, but I was also thinking, *What am I going to do if he wants some money?* I wasn't terribly worried about the "gun" because it wasn't illegal to carry one then, especially one that didn't actually shoot bullets.

One of those rare flashes of brilliance hit me as I got to the inspector.

"Hey," I said, "how the heck are you? It's been awhile since I saw you last . . . weren't you the inspector who took care of us when I was through here last with The Beach Boys?" They had been through Toronto more than once since I started working with Irving, but of course, never with me.

For some reason, maybe because I said "Beach Boys," he said, "Yeah . . . that was me. Good to see you again." With that, he put the tape across my attaché case and the other bags and I was home free.

I SEE MONTREAL AND MORE

Back on the airplane, my cribbage companion asked if I had ever been to Montreal before, and I admitted I hadn't, but was really looking forward to seeing the city.

She said, "You should never have to see Montreal for the first time without someone who knows it. I'd take you myself, but I'm engaged to be married. Don't get off the plane without talking to me."

Before we landed, she gave me a telephone number to call, saying that she would contact the person as soon as we got off the airplane. I gave her the name of the hotel where I was staying just in case we missed connections. The name and number was that of a German girl, also a stewardess with Air Canada.

As I was walking towards the baggage claim, the stewardess came running after me, shoving another piece of paper into my hand on which she had written a different name and telephone number. "Call this number first. She's available for tonight. The other number—the one I gave you on the plane—is for tomorrow."

I got to my hotel, checked in, tossed my jacket on the bed, made my telephone call to an English stewardess, arranged dinner, took down directions to her apartment, and went for a walk. The air was crisp, cold, and clean. It felt so good that I walked for about an hour jacketless, although the temperature couldn't have been much higher than low-forties.

The English stewardess lived in a high-rise on the other side of the Ottawa River, part of a large group of apartment buildings called Bellarive. Her apartment was near the top floor, high enough so that there was a clear view from her balcony all the way to the city and the St. Lawrence River. She fed me a couple of drinks and took me back into Old Town for dinner, where we watched the ocean-going freighters making their way down the St. Lawrence River. I made a lunch date with her for the day after my dinner with the German girl.

The next night, my German date came to my hotel to pick me up, and we dined and danced there, took a walk, and finished the night at an English pub. She was very beautiful, but not very communicative. I couldn't figure out what was expected of me, and while she plastered her body against mine as we danced and "necked," standard sex was pretty clearly out. After she left, I realized that she actually got herself off by rubbing her breasts against me while we were necking.

During the day, I had plenty to do locating and then driving to the radio stations, one of them a French station, and to the *Montreal*

Star, the *Montreal Gazette*, the French language paper, the *Montréal-Matin*, and of course, some shopping. I met my English date for a late lunch and bought her a small book of poems as a thank you for the nice time I had with her at dinner.

She said, "You know I wouldn't mind going to bed with you, but I'm getting married Sunday."

So, I said, "Okay, how about Saturday?"

She thought that might be a little tacky, but said she'd think about it.

I had hired Roy Cooper, a local publicist and promoter, by telephone before leaving Los Angeles, to handle the publicity, place ads, and monitor sales. It was Roy who suggested using the French language media, which was the primary reason that the event was a near sell out.

I paid him $500 for supervising everything including ticket sales at Place Ville Marie, a huge underground shopping mall. Actually, it was partly open at the top, and like much of Montreal, could be reached by subway. You could do virtually all your shopping in Montreal without ever having to come up into the winter cold.

From Montreal, I flew to St. John, Nova Scotia, where *our* Canadian dates were to start. That is, *I* flew to St. John, Nova Scotia; my luggage flew to St. Johns, Newfoundland. It caught up with me in Winnipeg, a couple of days later.

Before leaving Los Angeles, I made a deal with the only radio station in St. John that played rock and roll, to promote the date with a spot every fifteen minutes, and to handle ticket sales for 5 percent of the gross. The newspapers, the *Telegraph-Journal* and the *Evening Times Globe*, gave us tons of free publicity because I bought a couple of inexpensive ads.

Having finished my meetings with the newspapers and the radio station, I started walking towards the facility, which was actually the ice rink, where the local hockey team played, when a man stopped me on the street.

He asked, "You with The Beach Boys?"

I answered, "Yes. How did you know?"

He replied, "You sure as hell ain't from around here."

That I understood. My clothes were more stylish than his rubber boots and overalls. I also had a beard, and my hair was long. Everyone wore their hair over their ears in the late sixties, except in St. John.

The rink, I had been assured on the telephone, would accommodate 4,000 people, and I wanted to see how. I had always wanted to do reserved seat performances, but it was impossible there because there weren't enough portable folding chairs available in the entire city.

I walked into the rink and found the manger. "Where are you going to put 4,000 people?" I asked. "There can't be more than 2,500 seats in the stands."

"That's right," he said, "we'll sit 'em on the floor."

I said, "There's ice there. Won't they freeze their asses off?"

"Nope. I'll cover the ice with boards and they'll bring cushions. We've done it before." I took him at his word and flew out of town. There was no way I could stay overnight there. I never even checked to see if there was a hotel in town.

In Halifax, which was essentially just across the Bay of Fundy from St. John, I had set another 5 percent radio station deal while I was still in Los Angeles. Within a day, I started getting telephone calls from another station, CHNS, which also wanted the date. I told them I already had a deal, but they offered to top it. I said, "How can you do better than 5 percent?"

They said, "We'll do it for free."

I said, "They offered to run the ticket sales."

"Okay," they said, "We'll handle that too, and we'll be on the air every fifteen minutes, twenty-four hours a day pushing the concert." It created a little problem, but I got out of the first commitment by offering to buy some air time. Not only did CHNS plug the show every fifteen minutes, but the time breaks were announced as "Beach Boy Time," and the news was called "Your Beach Boy News." Everything they did carried the tag, "Beach Boys."

Ottawa was going well and presented no problems. I spent a few hours there making stops at the *Ottawa Journal*, the *Ottawa Citizen*, and *Le Droit*, the French paper, checked in with Harvey Glatt, who owned the Treble Clef music stores and handled our publicity and ticket sales. I wandered around the city for an hour or so, and then caught an airplane back to Los Angeles.

CHAPTER TWENTY-ONE:
It's Fun to Visit a Foreign Country

Even though we still hadn't received a dime of our deposit money from the Canadian promoter, we got ready to start our tour. By that time, we really had no choice, having booked a whole tour around his dates. Dick said, "We'll just have to take over his box offices." I agreed, and we headed to St. John for our own show.

As expected, the date was a winner. They had never before had a "name" act play in St. John. We got there for the late afternoon concert in time to see the doors open and the crowd rush to find places on the floor. The first person in line was a man about fifty years old, which confirmed my feeling that The Beach Boys appealed to a very wide audience. One of the things that always amazed me was the number of pre-teens in our audiences, which meant that The Beach Boys' music had staying power, not just with the age group that grew up with them. Although The Beach Boys were the first major rock act ever to play in St. John, within the next few months, other groups, obviously having heard of our success, began booking the town.

THE GOVERNMENT ATTACKS US

After the concert, Dick was busy reconciling the box office when I was approached by a man who identified himself as a representative of the Revenue Taxation Division of the federal government. He wanted 15 percent of the gross off the top, which we didn't want to give him, primarily as we were operating with no cash and were relying on each night's income to keep going. I managed to talk the revenue agent out of it. More like "double-talk" him out of it, convincing him that in all the years we had worked in Canada, we never paid taxes. I had no idea whether or not that was true.

In the meantime, while I was with the tax man, Dick's reconciliation of the box office showed that there was a shortage. Since the radio station had taken the responsibility for the money, they dropped their request for 5 percent of the gross for promoting the show.

Immediately after the St. John concert, we flew across the Bay of Fundy to Halifax. No sooner were we in the air than Dick asked me to check his figures for the box office, which I did, only to discover that not only was it not short, but there was an overage of about $60. We were reminded about Dick and his math, and so we decided to forget about it and just keep the money.

The radio station in Halifax provided cars to drive us to the hotel, where we were greeted by at least a couple hundred fans. Mike asked one particularly attractive young lady who was hanging tightly on to his arm if there was a Chinese restaurant nearby that might be open. She knew of a place and volunteered to drive three of us and two of her girlfriends there. It was more than a little cramped in her Ford Mustang, but some of the best times I've ever had were in very tight quarters. We drove up just as it was closing. An old Chinese was in the process of locking up when I jumped out of the car and ran to the door. He waved me away, but I used the more or less universal signal for begging, with my palms placed together as in prayer.

I indicated as best I could, in what I hoped would pass for understandable sign language, that I was hungry; that we were all hungry. Mike joined me, looking as desperate as he could. Then, Bruce and then the three girls joined in. The old man moved away from the door and we thought we were out of luck, but he returned a few seconds later, let us in, and led the way to a table.

He had gone to confer with his son, who came out of the office or wherever he was, and suggested that we let him prepare a special meal that was not featured on the menus. That was fine with us; we just wanted food. He asked if chicken dishes were all right, which it was, and when he finished cooking, he joined us for dinner. His father, who barely spoke English, had no idea who The Beach Boys were, but the son knew all about the concert and explained to the old man that he should be honored that some of them were gracing their table. We offered him tickets to the show and he took them.

Halifax is practically an island with only a narrow strip of land about ten miles wide at the north end connecting it to New Brunswick. I referred to Halifax as being "across the Bay of Fundy, and in fact, it essentially is. It is actually located on the Atlantic Ocean side of Nova Scotia at a point where only about twenty-five miles of land separates the Bay of Fundy from the Atlantic. The Bay was a water playground for the two provinces, as well as New Brunswick's access to the Atlantic. The radio station in Halifax operated a boat in the bay that reported weather and water conditions every half-hour on weekends for fishermen and water sports activities.

Having nothing to do in the morning and afternoon, some of The Beach Boys asked if they could go out on the boat for a couple of hours. The radio station was only too happy to oblige. They did interviews and took call-ins, and Dennis and Bruce read water condition reports and station breaks.

The bay was full of water skiers that day and Dennis managed to lure one of them over to the boat. He stopped alongside and climbed in. Dennis asked if he could use the water skis, to which the owner gladly agreed, and so Dennis spent the better part of an hour skimming over the waters of the Bay of Fundy in a white, sheared-velvet suit.

That night at the concert, another tax agent showed up at the box office, and I was able to convince him that we didn't have to pay the tax, explaining that we didn't have to pay it in St. John.

That particular agent said, "The way it has always been done is that American acts pay us here and our tax treaty with the United States allows them to deduct that amount from their US taxes." I wanted to avoid that at all costs. Since he didn't press the issue, we thought we'd managed a coup and that we'd get away with it for the entire tour. We really needed the cash since nothing was forthcoming from Nick.

The after-concert party that night went straight to my room. I know I didn't invite anyone, but there they were. Two deejays brought a couple of cases of beer and several females. The Beach Boys came in after they cleaned up and brought some people with them, mostly female.

The beer was going quickly, and someone suggested I call down to room service for some hard liquor. Room Service informed me that it was against government regulations to send bottles of whiskey to a room, so I asked if they could send up individual drinks.

Assured that they could do that, I ordered sixty-four shots of Canadian Club and sixty-four glasses of water chasers. Ten minutes later, a waiter arrived carrying a huge tray with sixty-four shot glasses and sixty-four small glasses of water. I signed for it and said, "Now go back downstairs and do it all over again."

The party was noisy, crazy, and fun, the most insane party we ever had while I was with them, with the exception of when we were in Spokane, Washington.

There was all that beer in bottles, but no one thought to bring an opener. Someone figured out it was possible to remove the bottle cap by hooking it into the latch on the bathroom door. One couple had taken themselves into the bathroom, locked the door and did what I can only surmise, but when they were done, the door jammed shut. The banging of beer bottle tops had thrown it out of kilter and they couldn't get it open. The only solution was for someone to remove the door hinge bolts to let them out.

Dennis showed up with a banana cream pie and asked if he could hit me in the face with it. I said, "Are you out of your fucking mind? Come near me with that thing and I'll shove it down your shorts." He intelligently left me alone and I went back to some serious drinking and ineffective hitting on a couple of the ladies.

Suddenly, there was a loud "thwack" sound. I looked up and saw Bruce covered in banana cream pie. Dennis hit him square in the face. Bruce was not happy and went after Dennis, who did the smart thing by getting the hell out of my room.

There was banana cream pie everywhere on the walls, the floors, and even in my shoes. That was it for me. I threw everyone out and tried my best to clean up. The room smelled like a brewery had exploded. The carpeting was sticky with beer that Dennis sprayed around the room earlier in the evening, and the bathroom door was in the tub, with the hinge pins nowhere to be found. I had to go around to two other rooms and remove one pin from each of their bathroom doors to put mine back up.

I realized there was no way I could sleep in the room because of the odor, not the mess. I opened the window to the cold, late fall air, set the bottles and glasses in the hall, emptied my shoes of banana cream pie, and ignored the goo on the walls. I propped the door open to create a draft, letting the wind blow through the room, and went for a walk around town for an hour, hoping the smell would go away, which it did.

The next morning, while we were preparing to leave, I got a telephone call from Winnipeg. The Canadian National Revenue Taxation Division wanted to talk to me in person. I got as much information from them as I could on the telephone concerning the tax codes and why they insisted on taking their cut from each show. Obviously, there was no way I was going to talk them out of it from Halifax.

Fortunately, we were scheduled for two or three dates back in the United States, and while Dick went there, I flew back to Los Angeles, after first making a call to Nick to have a copy of the Canadian–US tax treaty ready for me. Before I checked out, I informed the hotel desk that my room might present a small cleaning problem. I suggested they call in a carpet cleaning company and send the bill to our office. I would see to it personally that it was paid as soon as the tour ended.

CHAPTER TWENTY-TWO:
I Go Head to Head with the Canadian Government

Nick was an accountant, but not a CPA at that time because he had never been able to pass his exams. When we were back in Los Angeles, I asked him if he had read through the tax code and found any loopholes. He either hadn't read it or couldn't understand it, and he offered no solution other than telling me that I had to keep the Canadian government from taking the money.

I sat down with the tax code and read it very carefully from beginning to end, not understanding most of it. However, the section I decided to contest was right up front: Section 2-205 of the Assessments Guide. I returned to Winnipeg after spending a day and a half in Los Angeles, ready to do battle.

I met with two Assessors in their office and listened while they told me that the government had always collected tax from foreign groups on the gross of each date, or that alternately, we could estimate our total gross and give them a check up front. They explained that in the long run, it wouldn't cost us anything extra because we would get it back by deducting the amount we paid them when we filed our United States taxes. I didn't want to look like we were in dire financial straits, even though we were, so I had to argue my point along other lines.

The section of the treaty I contested had to do with something called a "permanent establishment." My position was that the government misinterpreted the intent of the section; that there was no way they could construe our group as being a permanent anything in Canada. I argued that we had no permanent base there, no Canadian record company connection, and were merely passing through with stops along the way.

I also argued that we did not maintain offices of any kind, had no storage facilities or equipment anywhere in Canada, and that our sound equipment was being flown in and out of each city. We were rarely in any city more than a day or two, and I pointed out that the main reason we were in Canada in the first place was not so much to make money—a really terrible lie—but for publicity reasons to increase the sales of our records in Canada, on which we *did* pay taxes. When I saw that point seeming to get a slightly positive reaction, I made it the main thrust of my argument. When pressed, I could talk as though I knew something about the law (or most anything else). I used words like "whereas" and "shall" (instead of "will") and it sounded pretty good. Also, I had no intention of giving in under any circumstances, unless it meant going to jail or something equally dire. After at least three hours, the two Assessors sat back and said that they guessed I was right, that they had never looked at it that way. What I told them made sense.

I said, "Great, and now that we're all done, do you have any kids who'd like to go to the concert? I didn't want to offer them to you before because then it would look like I was trying to bribe you."

They both had children of the appropriate age, so I gave them a couple of tickets and some for themselves, as well. I asked if they would give me a letter stating their new position just in case we ran into any more zealous tax collectors. They assured me it would be ready the next day if I cared to pick it up.

Very content with myself, I hurried back to the hotel and called Nick. I told him the good news and went down to the bar to celebrate. After three or four belts, I went back to my room only to find the message light on my telephone blinking. The Canadian Tax Division wanted me back the next day to explain it all over again to the top man in the department.

At nine the next morning, I was all primed for the meeting, hoping I could recall what I said the day before. The problem with speaking off the top of my head was that I didn't always remember what I'd said. I generally preferred to speak without notes, with only a general idea of what I was going to say. Usually, when I spoke, it involved something like emceeing a concert, talking about something with which I'm very familiar, or making a money pitch for some charity, but once I say my piece, it's pretty much wiped from my memory. Once I say it, it's gone.

I was ushered into the office of Mike Krutish, accompanied by the two Assessors with whom I had spent the previous day. I was introduced and told to, "Explain your position the way you presented it to us yesterday."

The end result of another two hours of discussing the treaty and arguing semantics was that the top man in the tax department saw my side and waived collection of taxes from our concert income even the four dates of the Canadian producer, although at first, they wanted that because *he* was a permanent establishment in Canada. Then, I offered *him* tickets, too, again saying that I waited so as not to create the impression I was trying to bribe him. I had my letter before I left the office.

I REJOIN THE TOUR AND WE VISIT EXPO '67

I flew back to Montreal that evening to await the arrival of The Beach Boys, feeling very proud of myself. I think The Beach Boys couldn't have cared less. They expected nothing less of me, and I didn't expect them to tell me that I had done a good job.

I made reservations for everyone at the Bonaventure Hotel because I liked the look of it when I was there on my previous trip. The hotel part of the building began on the seventeenth floor, the first sixteen being offices. The elevators opened to a thirty-foot wide lobby that led to the registration desk.

There were windows on both sides facing gardens replete with real grass, flowers, and flowing streams. On the right side was a very large swimming pool, and even though it was late fall, the sun was bright and the pool was protected from the wind. Everyone headed there for sunning or swimming as soon as they settled in their rooms.

The interesting thing about that hotel was the location of the rooms. Turning right or left off the center hall, which also contained a night club, restaurant, coffee shop, and the usual gift/notions store, you would go up or down what amounted to half a floor. All the rooms had windows facing the gardens or the pool. The sky was sparkling and brilliant blue, the air pure, sweet, and wonderfully free of pollutants, and the pool was too inviting to pass up.

Below the building were two levels of underground shops, and well below that, the subway. I spent some of my time in the stores after a quick visit to the box office and to Roy Cooper's office. We were not going to sell out, but sales were up to about 70 percent with a day to go. When we projected the date, we figured it would be profitable at 60 percent, so we weren't unhappy.

The year before, Montreal had been the hub of excitement for Canada. It was the year of Expo '67. Although the Expo was over, the grounds were still open. Most of the states and countries had left their buildings as permanent exhibits, and most of the midway rides were operating, making the grounds a more or less permanent amusement park. The Beach Boys wanted to go.

The morning of our concert, we piled into a couple of cabs and drove over. Expo was on an island and made an impressive sight as we approached over a bridge. Once on the grounds, we headed for the office to see if we might hire a guide since our time was limited. They were not only kind enough to provide a guide, but they gave us golf carts to drive so we could get through the park quicker.

We toured many of the buildings, spending more time in the US Pavilion than the others, and took in as much as humanly possible in the short time we had. However, we did find time to ride the roller coaster. In fact, we rode it again and again. When we returned the carts, the office manager said we could catch the subway just outside the park and it would take us directly to the hotel. Well, we *had* to do that.

We rode down the longest, steepest escalator I have ever seen to the subway platform, but couldn't find a sign for our train. Finally, someone saw we were obviously confused and came to our rescue, directing us down another long, steep escalator ride to another level that we had no idea existed. We took a fast ride to the hotel. Subway cars in Montreal rode on rubber wheels and the ride was eerily silent for a subway.

Back at the hotel, we rode up two more of the longest, steepest escalators I have even seen and past the shops to the building ground floor.

After Montreal, we played Ottawa, an uneventful but profitable date, and flew out the same night for Winnipeg and the start of the four dates for our Canadian promoter. The following afternoon, Dick and I did our usual check of the auditorium and then checked with Bill and Ed Gee of Celebrity Box Office to see how things were going, and whether the promoter had given them any trouble. Since everything was under control, we said we'd see them at the hall that night.

WE CONFRONT THE CANADIAN

He still hadn't met the promoter, who was obviously staying clear of us. We had to know we'd see him at the concert that night. About an hour before show time, Dick and I went to the auditorium box office, checked in with Bill and Ed, and said, "Where's the promoter?" They pointed to a well-dressed young man, perhaps in his mid-thirties, sitting in a corner, and they said, "That's him."

We introduced ourselves and said, "We'll take over the box office if you don't mind, just to make sure we get our money."

Dick said, "Did you bring your gun, Jack?"

"I sure did," I answered, putting my attaché case on the counter and opening it so that the very expensive holster with the very cheap "starter" pistol was in plain sight. "25-caliber," I explained to the promoter.

He took one look at the gun and said, "Anything you guys want is okay with me."

At the end of the evening, which was successful, we took all our money for the date plus almost everything else in the till. We decided to give the promoter something over the highest even dollar, which came to $1.16 in Canadian currency.

In our next stop at Edmonton, we had a commitment with the sponsoring radio station for a "lunch with a Beach Boy" promotion, recruiting Bruce Johnston for the date. The girl who won the contest was so excited she could hardly talk, especially when Dennis, Carl, and Alan joined us.

We all met in the revolving restaurant at the top of the hotel, which afforded us a marvelous view of the city. Pointing out in the distance, I asked one of our deejays what I was looking at. He said it was a ski jump. Ski jumps in Canada are not unusual, but that one was over the highway. The lunch went well, but before very long, Bruce started feeling queasy, and pretty soon, we were all feeling a little out of sorts. My only explanation was that I thought the revolving restaurant might have been revolving a little too fast.

In Edmonton, I took Alan and Bruce to a local television show for an interview. When we arrived, the host was in already on the air in conversation with a very obviously "swish" female impersonator, who was performing locally.

The host asked, "Do you have any children?"

His guest answered, "Actually, I do. I have a son."

To which the host responded, "Are you teaching him the act?"

The man said as patiently as he could, "It's something you have to be born with." I don't think the host ever understood.

That night, we once again ran the box office while the promoter went out front to watch the show. "You don't mind, do you?" he asked. "I've never seen them live." We again took all the money except for about a $1.75, which we once again gave to the promoter.

As we were still carrying the cash from the Winnipeg date in our cases, we put the money from both shows in a couple of bank bags, each marked with big dollar signs (no kidding) and took them back to our rooms. The next morning, Dick and I wandered the streets of Edmonton, window shopping, with the bags slung casually over our shoulders, while we waited for a bank to open.

The third of the promoter's dates, in Regina, went as did the first two, and once again, we took all but a couple of dollars. So far, the promoter was making a lot of money, but didn't have any of it, except of course, for something less than four Canadian dollars. We had a lot more than was due us, but Dick and I were having a good time, and that guy wasn't complaining. By then, we were giving some thought to keeping it all and telling him to screw off, but eventually decided against that. I think he really thought I might shoot him and was willing to trade his life for any financial losses.

The last date in Vancouver was again very successful. That night after the concert, Dick and I sat in the box office saying things like, "Do you suppose we should charge him for the bus we hired? What else can we deduct?" Finally, having had enough of the silly game, and since we were anxious to get back to the hotel, we settled up and give him his profits. We got all our money, including our percentages, and he still came away a very neat profit. As we were walking out of the box office, he called after us, "Do you think we could do this again next year?" Dick and I laughed all the way to the hotel.

CHAPTER TWENTY-THREE:
Memories of My Last Months with The Boys

I finally left American Productions and The Beach Boys in April 1969, a little more than a year after I started, but not before accumulating a few more memories, some of which are perhaps worth mentioning:

There was another television appearance, this time in Los Angeles. *The Kraft Music Hall* had become *The Kraft Comedy Hour*, and Don Adams, Kaye Ballard, and Don Rickles were booked to headline the show. The Beach Boys were asked to do two songs as their "Special Guest Stars."

People who pay attention to that sort of thing know that Adams and Rickles spent a good part of their careers breaking up one another on stage and in public. This would turn out to be no different. Their shtick on this show was recreating memorable scenes from famous movies in comedic, stupid ways.

One scene called for Kaye to throw a pie at Don Adams, who was to duck and let it hit Don Rickles. On the first take, she aimed too low and hit Adams, which meant a break while they cleaned up and washed him off, combed and dried his hair, and mopped the stage. From then on, it was chaos. She hit Adams, she hit Rickles on the top of the head, she hit him in the suit, and Rickles tried ducking down into it. Each inaccurate toss calling for a break while they once again washed hair, cleaned suits, and mopped the stage.

We had an eight o'clock call to tape two songs, but got there early to watch the stars at work. The producers figured that Kaye, Adams, and Rickles should be pretty close to finished by that time, since they started early. By eight o'clock, The Beach Boys had been through make-up and we were all sitting in the bleachers watching, laughing, and waiting our turn.

At eight, they were nowhere near ready for us. Hour after hour passed, as the trio continued to screw up and we continued to be their best (and only) audience. The stars finally decided to call it quits around three o'clock in the morning and finish the next night. They left and we waited again, while the crew reset the stage for the first of The Beach Boys songs. It was four o'clock in the morning by the time they were ready, but The Beach Boys did a great job and the technicians finally got the song on tape.

Of course, we had to come back the next night to tape the second song, and again they had to wait for the stars to finish their turn. Our call that time was for nine o'clock because the stars couldn't start shooting and the crew couldn't start working until four in the afternoon, which had something to do with a union requirement for a "twelve-hour turnaround," I believe.

Once again, we were all there early. The Beach Boys went through the make-up department again, sat around in the green room watching the taping on a television set for awhile, and then ended up back in the bleachers, while Kay, Adams, and Rickles continued to screw up one bit after another to their seemingly never-ending self-amusement. What the hell, when they were through *they* could go home. That time, they finally got to The Beach Boys around two o'clock in the morning.

A CHANGE OF HEART

On our next tour, we were to leave Akron, Ohio right after a show and drive into Cleveland, where we would stay overnight, and then fly to Hartford, Connecticut late the next morning.

However, while the opening act was on stage, The Beach Boys talked it over among themselves and voted to go directly to Hartford that night instead, if at all possible. So, once I got the second half of the show under way, I contacted the airlines and found that there was indeed a flight out of Cleveland, but in order to make it, we'd really have to hustle. I gave them the option of driving like hell to make it or staying in Cleveland; they opted for Hartford.

I changed our hotel reservations in Hartford, arranged to drop the rental cars at the airport curb and leave the keys on the car rental counter. I moved three vehicles just outside the auditorium back entrance for a fast getaway.

I explained once more that we had a little more than thirty-five minutes to make the thirty-five mile drive to the Cleveland airport. That would give us just enough time to check our bags and get on the airplane. There should have been no problem with averaging sixty miles an hour, especially at that hour. The road would be open and non-stop. However, it was going to be close.

I drove the lead car, I'm pretty sure Bruce drove the second, and I know Dennis drove the third. I admonished them that we had very little leeway and they had better keep up with me; that I would not wait for anyone who didn't arrive on time, and took off like the proverbial bat-out-of-hell for Cleveland.

I pulled into the airport and hustled everyone in my car through check-in and sent them ahead to the gate. Bruce pulled up a few moments later and they raced off, but Dennis was nowhere to be seen. I waited five minutes and then left. Needless to say, Dennis did not make it.

The flight to Hartford was a short one, and when we arrived at the hotel, there was a message at the reservations desk from Dennis. I called the number he left—a pay telephone at the Cleveland airport.

"I told you to keep up or I'd leave you," I said.

Dennis was surprisingly contrite. He apologized and asked, "What should I do now?"

I said, "Find the nearest hotel; there has to be one at the airport, check in and have the desk clerk call me for a credit card number, and then call me back in an hour."

I called the airline and was able to re-book Dennis and his passengers on the morning airplane to Hartford. You could do that easily in those days and the ticket agents were very cordial and helpful. Of course, we were flying first class, and first class passengers always got special treatment, anyway.

HUSTLING THROUGH FLORIDA

Another trip had us doubling up on dates in Florida. Once again, we hired limousines to send the acts ahead as they finished, this time from Tampa/St. Petersburg to Sarasota. The chartered Viscount dropped us in Tampa and then flew ahead to meet us in Sarasota for a late night flight into Miami Beach.

As soon as The Beach Boys finished their last song, I hustled everyone off stage into the back seat of a waiting limo—all but Mike Love, who found a young girl to drive him. I took a seat in front with a roadie for The Grass Roots, who were opening for us on that trip. Stuffed into the back seat and jump seat were Dennis, Alan, Carl, and Bruce.

We were on the road about five minutes when I heard a strange noise emanating from the back seat. I turned around and for the first time realized there was a young woman with us.

She was kneeling in front of Dennis, giving him head. Ignoring them was difficult, if for no other reason than the intensity and passion she brought to the job. Ignoring them became *impossible* once she and Dennis changed places so he could engage in a little sexual intercourse with her. When Dennis finished, he switched places with whoever had been sitting next to the young lady, who then got up off her back to take a better position for another blow job. Alan Jardine was third in line and finished a few seconds before the driver pulled off the highway to get gas.

Everyone got out to stretch their legs. It was, after all, a little cramped in the back seat. I turned to Alan, who like the others, was wearing a white, crushed velour suit. He had removed the jacket earlier, and was dressed only in his pants, shirt, shoes, and socks.

I said, "It's a good thing we didn't drive straight through and have to go right on stage."

"Why," he asked.

"Because you put your pants back on inside-out."

We finally arrived a short time later in Sarasota, before the young lady, who happened to be a nurse, was able to take care of *everyone*, although she was certainly willing enough. Unfortunately, we ran out of time.

We all went into what passed for a dressing room, where I had a few moments to talk with her and invite her—at the direction of my employers—to go on with us to Miami. I also asked her if her jaws didn't get tired.

She answered, "███████████████████" I suggested

that if she came with us, she could finish the job she started, but she declined, explaining, "I couldn't do that, my mother would worry."

I said, "What do you think she'd be doing if she knew where you are and what you've been doing up to now?"

She replied, "I guess she'd worry."

I think she managed to take care of one or two members of the Grass Roots before she left for the airport to catch her airplane back home, but she didn't have time to do everyone. Out of gratitude, I suppose, The Beach Boys paid her air fare back to Tampa.

I HAVE MY SAY ABOUT DRUG USE

Let me say that since I left the group back in 1969, I have heard and read all sorts of comments about the boys, frequently about their drug use. I think that may have been because of Brian's problems. Dennis very likely abused all sorts of substances at one time or another, but only once did he do anything when we were on the road together, and I have already chronicled that.

After a concert, if someone provided the grass, they might have all gone back to the hotel and smoked, but never *before* a concert, and only rarely after. Marijuana was the extent of their drug use during the more than three years (two-and-a-half with Irving Granz) that I was associated closely with them.

There was a time when they decided it was very "in" to drink wine, usually a good red. We were doing two performances somewhere, perhaps Omaha, Nebraska, when eight of us decided to have dinner between shows. We were directed to what was considered a fine restaurant near the theater and naturally ordered a couple of bottles for the table. Finishing them, we ordered one more and finally, one last bottle to wind up the dinner.

The waitress, a charmer if I ever met one, came up and said to me, "Hey, you, we're out of red wine."

I said, "How could you possibly be out red wine, you must serve more than four bottles a night. Please, do me a favor and go look again."

"Okay," she said, returning a few moments later with a bottle in her hand. "Is this red wine?"

I looked at the label. "It clearly says Rosé. How could it be red wine?"

"Do you want it or not?" she asked.

The Beach Boys agreed to take it, whereupon she handed me the bottle and a corkscrew and said, "Here, you open it." I carried that corkscrew with me for several years before leaving it somewhere.

CARL TAKES OVER

I think I was closer to Dennis and Bruce than any of the others, although I felt very close to Mike and spent some time at his home in Santa Barbara on more than one occasion after I resigned. Carl was just too young, and frequently acted his age.

Then, too, he initially resisted taking over as "leader" of the group, I suspect in deference to Brian, but the job became his by default after Mike, Dennis, and Alan more or less elected him. He finally accepted the role, although he wasn't sure he could do it. Other writers of The Beach Boys' history have said that Carl just assumed the role of leader, but the truth is that he had to be pressured into it.

When it finally came to recording their next album, everyone from Nick on down told Carl he would have to be the producer, because Brian surely wasn't going to be able to handle the job and none of the other members of the group seemed to want it. Mostly, Carl was pushed into it to help build his self-confidence as titular head of the group. Besides, he was going to have a lot of help from everyone and probably couldn't have screwed up if he tried. Bruce, being a highly trained musician and excellent writer and producer in his own right, could have done it easily, but he was not at that time an official Beach Boy, in that he was an employee being paid by the job. As I said, Brian was pretty much incommunicado.

I recall the session when they recorded "Heroes and Villains" at a small studio in North Hollywood. The song was originally to be a part of the *Smile* album, which was never finished although many, if not all, the music tracks were on tape already and stored at our office.

"Heroes and Villains" was the lead song on the *Smiley Smile* album, which featured other songs also intended for *Smile*, plus a re-release of "Good Vibrations."

When I got to the studio, Carl and Van Dyke Parks were trying to reconstruct the original lyrics for "Heroes and Villains," which Van Dyke wrote. I guess no one had ever written them down in their entirety, or even more likely, could find them.

Although it was a good album, *Smiley Smile*, along with *Friends* and *Wild Honey*, did not get the recognition they deserved. The *20/20* album did fairly well, and that brings to mind yet another story that is interesting only because it was indicative of the way record promotions for The Beach Boys was being handled at that time.

I ADD ANOTHER ROLE TO PLAY

We were planning a Texas tour and wanted a heavy push from Capitol Records throughout the state. Capitol was telephoning our office daily from their Hollywood headquarters on Vine Street, with reports on album play on stations around the country, but I never quite trusted them.

I knew one of the promotion people at Capitol and he let me use his WATS (Wide Area Telephone Service) line while he was out at lunch. I went in every day and called all the Texas radio stations. It didn't take long to discover that Capitol's reports of radio station activity were mostly fabrications. Some of the station managers and programmers I spoke with didn't even have the record, as was the case in Dallas, a very important market for us, both in record sales and concerts. A few stations had just received it in the mail, but had nothing on their play list yet. Some had programmed a couple of songs, but only as "extras."

I gathered a couple dozen albums, got on an airplane, flew to Dallas, rented a car, and worked my way down the state to Corpus Christi on the Gulf, and then over to Houston, from which I flew back to Los Angeles. I stopped at every radio station I could find, including colleges in Waco (Baylor University) and Austin (University of Texas).

Before I left for Dallas, I called the Capitol promo man there and asked him to meet me at the #1 rock and roll radio station. I called the station as soon as I arrived in town, but the Capitol promotion man still hadn't delivered a record, and to make matters worse, he didn't even bother to show up for the meeting. I played the album for the program manager and he agreed to program two of the songs.

At every stop, stations put one or more songs on their play list, and at every stop, I found that Capitol Records promo people hardly ever stopped by, and in no case did anyone actually approach them to request air time for any particular cut on the album. Incidentally, I was so naive about record promotion, I never even offered to buy anyone lunch, never offered anyone payola of any kind, and in fact, got station people to take *me* to lunch. At one station, I even recorded a station promo spot.

I don't mean to imply that Capitol promotion men did that with every record and for every act because I can only speak for the evidence I found when I went out and checked on *20/20*.

Looking at the album jacket recently brought back memories of the mastering sessions at Capitol. The Beach Boys frequently preferred to work late at night, and I was there two or three times. It seemed as though everyone took a turn at producing a cut, with Steve Desper, our own engineer/sound man, at the console. No one had been able to satisfactorily master *All I Want to Do*, a song written and performed by Dennis. Carl turned to me and said, "Do you want to try?" I answered, "Why not?"

The problem, as I saw it, was that Dennis frequently drifted off key, particularly on high notes, and it sounded awful. I covered his bad notes by bringing up the music volume.

I left early one night when they were working at Capitol Records studio and missed the most unusual mastering session of them all. I was told that during a break around two o'clock in the morning, Dennis wandered out onto Vine Street in front of Capitol. He met a young lady whom he charmed, brought her inside, and had his way with her as she lay back on the console. He held a microphone on either side of her head to record her ecstasy in stereo. Then, he mastered the sound into the end of the record at what he described as a subliminal level.

Dennis believed that if people heard the subliminal sounds of people engaged in sex, it would prompt them to do the same. He thought that turned-on people would be so busy making love that they wouldn't fight with one another. Who knows, maybe he had a point.

I told that story to the deejays at every station and then played the cut with all the bass removed and the treble up high. I will not say as an absolute certainty that the sexual event actually happened because I was not there, and I will not say those sounds could truly be heard, but I *will* say that every jock I played it for swore he could hear the young lady in the throes of orgasm.

CHAPTER TWENTY-FOUR:

Winding Down My Stint with The Beach Boys

On the road, I spent more time with Bruce Johnston or Dick Duryea than anyone else, and of course, when I took on Dick's job after his problems with Dennis and Mike, if I went to dinner with anyone, it was generally Bruce. He was very bright, intellectual, and an excellent, classically-trained pianist, a better than average singer, and a composer and record producer of considerable talent. He frequently recorded and produced with Terry Melcher, son of Doris Day, both before and after he joined The Beach Boys. Some of the songs on their albums are his, and he wrote the mega-hit, "I Write the Songs."

He told me he learned to play the bass in one night in 1964 in a hotel room in New Orleans, when he joined the group replacing Brian Wilson, who was no longer touring. Bruce was paid by the performance. He remained in that position until some time after I resigned. I ran into him after they made him a partner and he told me he was much better off financially when he was just working for them.

Visiting his apartment one afternoon, he told me that because he was young, and with insurance rates being what they were for a single male, under thirty, he decided against owning a car. He rented a car whenever he needed one, and used a motorcycle for his general transportation. I know he bought stocks as investments, and certainly seemed to be savvy about the market.

I have spoken to Bruce only a few times over the last twenty-five or so years, once, shortly after Dennis died and in 1999, when someone I met gave me his telephone number in Montecito, California. I was never able to contact any other members of the group after Dennis's accident, as by then, I had lost touch with them all.

Mike, for all his quirkiness, proved to be very bright and in ways one might not expect. He was a student of history and, as I have mentioned, a knowledgeable collector of Americana.

Dick Duryea was also a collector of antiquity, and we went looking on a few occasions. Somewhere in the northwest, perhaps Seattle, he located a small Tiffany lamp, but that's about all I can recall finding while we were traveling together, except once when I bought a pair of antique railroad lamps of some kind, which ended up stored away in the garage, never to be seen again.

Dick also quit The Beach Boys, not long after I left. He was involved in a land acquisition deal for which he expected to get a percentage. There might have been arguments over the deal that had to do with his leaving, and he didn't leave under happy circumstances, according to a conversation I had with Margaret Adler late in 1999. I can only conjecture that Nick sided with The Beach Boys when they objected to the percentage Dick expected for putting the deal together.

Frequently, we hired additional musicians for a tour. Mike Kowalski was with us often, his primary function being the replacement drummer when Dennis came down from the riser to sing. When Mike wasn't playing drums, he played the tambourine or congas, and was certainly the highest-paid tambourine player in the country. I know we paid him $300 a week in 1968 when he went on the European tour.

We generally brought along a bass player, Eddie Carter, because Bruce couldn't play organ and bass at the same time. Al Jardine was at one time the bass player, but by the time I joined the group, he was playing only rhythm guitar. Carl played lead guitar and Mike, of course, played the Theremin, although I think he played a couple of notes on a saxophone once or twice on early albums. Eddie was a better bassist than Bruce, but then that was his instrument.

John D'Andrea, who later went on to considerable success as a composer and conductor, more than once put together horn sections for us. Sal Marquez, a fantastic trumpet player, later had his own jazz group, worked steadily as a studio and television musician, and was also a fairly regular performer with us.

Doug, Darryl, and Dennis Dragon, a trio of brothers comes to mind because they individually traveled with us from time to time. At least once, all of them were on the same trip. The sons of famed conductor Carmen Dragon, the brothers were all a little on the odd-ball side, but great traveling companions. Dennis was a drummer, joining us instead of Mike Kowalski. Doug played bass, and Darryl, later better-known as "The Captain" of The Captain and Tenille," played piano.

What I remember most about Darryl were his large brown eyes that always seemed watery. I kept asking him whether or not he was ill, but he always felt fine, until one day when I said, "You look terrific today, what's the matter?" That was the one day he wasn't feeling well.

Dennis had blond, curly hair over which he generally wore an army helmet or helmet liner. I think he must have worn it to bed. Whenever he removed it, his tight curls had molded into the shape of whichever helmet he was wearing. The brothers later formed a jazz trio and played around Los Angeles for awhile. Before Darryl met Toni, I imagine.

CARL BECOMES A CONVERSATIONALIST

Carl told me a story about himself and the other members of the group, prefacing it with a line about him not always being very smart. A very good friend of theirs was Danny Hutton, the leader of Three Dog Night, which was first called The Redwoods at the time Brian was going to produce an album for them. The group had considerable success initially, and then moderate success when they made a comeback several years later.

According to Carl, Danny came to them when they were first starting out and asked if The Beach Boys' company would manage them. Carl said, "Why would we want to manage you guys? I don't think you have a chance," or words to that effect.

Jon Parks told me about another of their miscalculations that probably cost them a ton of money. When The Beach Boys used a form of the Theremin in "Good Vibrations," it was made for them by Robert Moog, the man who also invented the synthesizer. Jon and someone else went to pick up the Theremin, but at that time, Moog told him he had built the synthesizer, but had no idea what to do with it. He was willing to give the invention to The Beach Boys if they would give him a percentage when and if they were able to market it. They turned him down.

I MAKE A NEW CONNECTION

One of the groups we hired on the road was The Sheep, a member of which was Jerry Goldstein. Jerry was also the leader of another group that did a short tour with us, and they had a big hit or two. I believe he had something to do with the song "Hang On Sloopy," which always seems to come up when Jerry's name was mentioned.

By 1969, Jerry was off the road and with a partner in a company then called Music Tours, Inc. Jerry and Steve Gold were in the business of producing and selling posters for rock and roll artists. Jerry called our office to make a deal with The Beach Boys.

I really didn't connect him with the groups when he called, but when he showed up in my office, we recognized one another and put everything together. We discussed a possible deal to produce a poster for them and came to an agreement in principle. We couldn't, at that time, agree on the financial aspect of the deal. I wanted more than they were willing to offer.

Before we could complete the deal, I had to hit the road to promote an upcoming tour, and turned everything over to Dick Duryea, who was a tougher negotiator than I. Things were pretty nearly finalized by the time I returned. I know Dick was out of the office when I met with Jerry to close the deal, but I don't think he was back in their good graces or traveling with the group again.

Jerry arrived with two other people in tow. He took a chair in front of me, while the other two took seats against the wall behind him. We kicked around his original offer and Dick's counter offer, but I wouldn't back down. Finally, Jerry turned to the people behind him, neither of whom had spoken a word to that point, whispered something, turned back to me, and agreed to our terms.

While Jerry was filling in some details on the contract, a voice from behind him spoke up. The voice had a character difficult to describe, but something akin to a two-tone fog horn and a growl, is as close as I can come.

"Why don't we hire this bum?" it rumbled.

"What would you say to that?" Jerry added.

"Well, I'll always listen. What'll you give me?"

The voice from the chair behind Jerry rumbled again, "I'll give ya a room with a window." Our building had no exterior windows.

"That's it?!" I exclaimed.

"I'll give ya a motorcycle," the voice grumbled.

"I don't know how to ride a motorcycle," I said.

"I'll teach ya," growled the voice.

"It's an interesting offer," I said. "I don't know how I can refuse, but I didn't hear anything about money. Give me a call when you get around to that."

We all signed the contract and they left. The next time I heard from Jerry was to get approval of the poster art, and then I did not hear from him again for about a month until when he called me once again at the office.

"Hey," he said, "it's Jerry. I wanted to talk to you about coming to work for us. Were you serious when you said you'd consider it?"

It was about that time when I began having more serious problems with Nick, trying to and not getting money to advance or promote our own dates, and then the problem with our promoter in Boston. I began to feel as though I ought to quit. Nick had lied to me on several occasions, he failed to provide funds for a proposed tour, and I didn't like the idea of just sitting around and collecting a pay check. I don't think The Beach Boys wanted me to quit—I don't know if they even knew how I felt—but it very likely didn't concern them one way or another.

I told Jerry that I certainly would consider talking to them whenever they wanted to talk dollars. Jerry asked me to come to his office on Canon Drive in Beverly Hills, where he, Steve Gold, and I could get together. We had a reasonably short meeting at which they offered me a substantial increase over what I was getting with The Beach Boys.

"Why do you want me to come here?" I asked.

"Well, you seem to be an organized person, and you know the souvenir sales business, and we need someone like you. We're making a lot of money, but don't know where it's going."

I said I would consider it and get back to them in a couple of weeks. When Nick and I had another run-in, my mind was made up. I wrote a letter to each of The Beach Boys explaining my decision and resigned. No one tried to talk me out of leaving except Dick, Lynette, Pat, and Kathy.

At that point, I felt there was no turning back. As much fun as I'd had on the road and even in the office, it wasn't going to be enough for me to stay. I couldn't continue arguing with Nick Grillo, and after what he did to my friend, Fred Taylor, in Boston, I wasn't even going to be able to talk to him. So, I packed up my gear, said my good-byes to the people I cared about, and walked out, although, as it turned out, I was not quite through with them.

ONE MORE THOUGHT

I have one more item about Brian, as well as everyone, but it was perhaps the only other time I spent with Brian. We were all invited to the opening of The Beatles animated film, *Yellow Submarine*, a premiere of some sort in Westwood Village. There was a line of cars heading for the theater, each stopping in turn to disgorge its passengers to the red carpet leading into the movie house. There were hundreds of people lined up outside the velvet ropes, as one rock star or movie star after another walked in. We were in line directly behind Brian's Rolls Royce. The valet shot forward to open the door for Brian and Marilyn, and then we pulled up in my little red Toyota. Everyone wondered, "Who the hell are they?" The valet who got my car must have been terribly embarrassed.

A REUNION WITH MY FORMER EMPLOYERS

The Beach Boys were appearing at the Delaware State Fair in Dover, and I went just to supervise the poster sales and do a little

PR work for the company. Besides, I figured I'd have a good time at the fair and get to spend two or three days with them.

I flew into Washington, DC, rented a car, and made the leisurely and scenic drive to Dover. I caught the shows each night and hung with them after.

One of the acts on the show was a "Chimp Act." Wandering around back stage, the chimps were lined up sitting on a fence. With a couple of The Beach Boys, I approached them. Two of the larger chimps were stretching out their arms toward us, sort of asking to be petted. I started toward them and was stopped by their trainers.

"I wouldn't do that," he said. "You can't trust them; just as likely to bite off your fingers."

"How do you control them?" I asked.

He reached into his back pocket and pulled out a blackjack, smacking it into his palm.

Shortly after I got back to Los Angeles, Jerry Goldstein asked me to invite The Beach Boys, as his guests, to Las Vegas, where Elvis Presley was making his second comeback. The group that went included Brian and Marilyn Wilson, Bruce Johnston and his date, Alan Jardine, Linda, my wife, and Jerry and his date. Bruce's lady friend was a friend of Sharon Tate's, who on that very weekend was murdered by the Charles Manson tribe.

Following the performance by Elvis, Bruce asked me to find out if they could go up to his suite for a visit. They were, after all, friendly. On my way to the telephone, I passed Glen Campbell and asked if he was going up to see Elvis.

He said, "Parker said no."

Nevertheless, I called the suite and spoke with Colonel Tom Parker, who was no more a Colonel than I was. It was the second time I had ever spoken with him. The first time was at the behest of Tats Nagashima, then the top music publisher and promoter in Japan. Tats asked me to make an offer for Presley. He would give Elvis $3 million dollars for three concerts over a period of thirty days in Japan. Parker said, "Tell him no thanks, we don't need money that bad."

DECISIONS, DECISIONS

Around that time, actor José Ferrer asked me to become his Personal Manager. I said, "Joe, I'll do it on three conditions. First, we do not sign any agreements because I want to be able to walk away from the job if I get mad at you, and I want you to be able to do the same thing. Besides, our friendship means more to me than whatever money I might make. Second, you have to pay my percentage."

He asked what that would be, and I said, "15 percent." He nodded. "And most important," I continued, "you have to listen to me. If I make a decision, I don't want you going behind my back and make me look stupid. I'm not going to commit you to anything without conferring with you, but if an offer doesn't make any sense to me, or if I think the property is a piece of crap, I'm going to reject it without ever bothering you. Oh, I'll tell you about it, but I won't send you the script. And I don't want you to ever deal with an agent or a producer directly. When it's called for, I'll be the bad guy, not you."

"Okay," he said. "I agree. Your friendship means a lot to me, too, and that's just the way I want it."

"One more thing," I said, "I don't want to be called a 'Personal Manager.' It sounds like you're too dumb to tie your own shoe laces. Let's just say were business associates." Joe thought that was a good idea, too.

My new relationship with Joe didn't end my involvement with Steve Gold, Jerry Goldstein, nor The Beach Boys. The Beach Boys and I spoke from time to time, mostly by accident, but one day Mike Love called me, ostensibly to see if I knew how to get in touch with a young lady named "Jovita," a name one is not likely to forget. She was a strikingly beautiful model I met some months earlier through an agent friend. The agent had mentioned my connection to The Beach Boys to her, and Jovita told me she knew Mike Love, apparently in the Biblical sense. She asked if I knew how to reach Mike, and I told her I did, whereupon she asked me to have Mike call her, which I did. Shortly after that, Mike changed his telephone number and I lost touch with him.

As it happened, I did have a new number for Jovita, and gave it to him. If he wanted to call her, that was his business. As I was no longer working for him, I didn't feel the need to set up his dates.

A RETURN TO THE CONCERT BUSINESS

Mike Love asked if I would be willing to produce two more concerts for The Beach Boys, which was the real reason behind the call.

Mike had formed a non-profit organization which he called The Love Foundation. He planned to do four concerts to raise money that he was going to use to do some sort of good works. I had no idea what good works he planned, but as he agreed to pay me 10 percent of the gross, I took on the job and set about finding a couple of locations.

Two other two dates were already set, one at California Polytechnic Institute, better known simply as Cal Poly, in San Luis Obispo, and the other at California State University at Santa Barbara, which is really in Goleta, but both were close to his Santa Barbara home. The home was in a beautifully rustic, heavily wooded setting at the edge of a cliff. The kitchen and yard overlooked the ocean and a nude beach, too far below to see anything worthwhile.

Originally, I had no intention of doing anything with the other two dates because Jon Parks, who had taken over some of my former duties with American Productions, was supposed to be handling them. That wasn't the way it turned out, however.

The first thing I did, before I got too heavily involved in production, was call my young friend, Mike Zugsmith, and ask if he wanted to produce the concerts with me. We would split the income, but mostly, we'd be doing it for fun. Mike was more than anxious as he had never produced a concert with an act as important as The Beach Boys.

We made deals with the University of California in Riverside and at UC Irvine, and then set about doing all the usual things that go along with producing a concert. That included everything from making deals with local radio stations, doing some advertising with The Beach Boy's money, to working out details with the schools.

In essence, the school would get The Beach Boys in concert in exchange for their promoting the dates, selling the tickets, and providing the facilities. As those were charity affairs, we had to get the radio stations to give us air time in exchange for using their call letters in all the advertising and promotion, and to get the schools to donate all their time and effort.

There was one more little detail to be ironed out. Mike Love's "foundation" had not yet been granted non-profit status by the state. Doing a "charity" event without certification could conceivably get him and The Beach Boys in some trouble. Jerry Brown, who was then Secretary of State (later Governor, and then Attorney General), was invited to join The Beach Boys and me for dinner at Musso and Frank, a very famous restaurant on Hollywood Boulevard. Afterwards, we all would go to The Beach Boys concert at the Hollywood Palladium.

As soon as we were seated in a large corner booth at the front of the restaurant, The Beach Boys began trying to make an impression. Mike Love began by ordering an excellent wine. After a bottle or two, Jerry (as he preferred to be called) turned to me and asked quietly, "Is it okay if I just have a beer?"

During the course of dinner, I asked him if there was anything he might do to facilitate the issuing of their non-profit status. That was the real reason I had been invited. After another swig of beer from the bottle, he turned to his secretary and said, "Take care of it in the morning." I didn't have to work very hard.

Both of our concert dates sold well because we were at two very good schools in reasonably affluent areas. At Riverside, we ordered in a variety of healthy foods to which The Beach Boys were more than partial. A trio of young people from a local health food restaurant was already laying out the food in the dressing room by the time The Beach Boys arrived. Everyone appeared to be in a good mood, but Dennis was particularly garrulous, which made me suspect that he had partaken of something other than healthy food before show time. Either that or he really was happy to see me again.

I mentioned sometime back that Dennis never gave me any trouble after the date at VPI, and that was true, until that night. Someone handed him a jug of wine as he came down from his drum riser for a vocal solo, but I walked out and took it out of his hands before he could take a drink.

He had no choice but to go to the microphone, where he sang his song before he came after me at the back of the stage. I could see he was upset, so I handed the wine to someone, walked towards him, and wrapped my arms around him, pinning his own arms at his sides, so he couldn't do anything. I remembered what he did to Dick Duryea who had somehow upset him.

"Now, Dennis," I said, "do you remember you once promised me you would never do anything like that on one of my shows?" It stopped him long enough to think about it and he said, "Okay, Jack, I won't."

Other than having Carl's guitar stolen from the dressing room, the date was uneventful as well as profitable for Mike's foundation. Curiously, the person who stole the guitar later called The Beach Boys office and offered to sell it back to Carl. They agreed to meet and Carl said he would pay whoever it was, but it was the police who kept the date and Carl got his guitar back.

UC Irvine was another good date, except that The Beach Boys were very late. The audience was getting restless and we had nothing to keep them occupied. I was getting a bit nervous.

We didn't have an opening act because The Beach Boys planned to play a full two-hour set, with a ten-minute intermission. Everything was set up on stage, waiting for their arrival, so I knew that when they finally arrived, they could start immediately. Still, I worried until a flash of inspiration solved the problem.

My son, Robert, who played keyboards, was working as a member of the stage crew, and I knew that Jason, one of the regular roadies, was a rock guitarist. I asked if anyone else from the road crew played and it happened that one was a drummer and another played bass, and so I sent them out to jam until The Beach Boys arrived. When they finally arrived I said to Carl, "Don't start tuning your guitar; it's already tuned. Just start playing before we have a riot."

Even though Mike Zugsmith and I supposedly had no involvement in the two other dates, we were invited to come and join the party before the UC Santa Barbara concert. My wife and son came along, too, and we all convened at Mike Love's home in Santa Barbara for drinks and hors d'oeuvres.

Mike was married again to a girl I first thought was the Mexican housekeeper. She did nothing but serve food and never spoke to anyone but Mike, who seemed more into giving orders than making requests. As far as I know, Mike never considered asking her to the show.

Jon Parks was supposed to produce that event, but he was nowhere to be found as show time approached, so Mike Zugsmith and I just took over until Jon arrived shortly before intermission.

That meant I could watch the second half with my wife and son. We were all back stage prior to the concert, waiting for Jon to show up; my son was giving a harmony lesson to Eddie Carter, the bass player, and we were just busy enjoying ourselves primarily because there was absolutely no pressure. When it came time to start the show, Mike and I just did what we did naturally.

THE MORE THINGS CHANGE THE MORE SOME THINGS STAY THE SAME

On December 28, 1983, Dennis drowned while diving from a friend's boat and trying to recover items that he had previously thrown overboard in fits of rage. I ran into Dennis once more before pretty much losing touch with everyone until Dennis's untimely death. That was only through Bruce Johnston when I called to have him convey my condolences to the brothers.

My last encounter with Dennis happened one night as I was returning home late from Goldstein and Gold's Beverly Hills office. Heading north over Benedict Canyon to the San Fernando Valley, I saw Dennis sitting on his motorcycle at the top of the hill, on Mulholland Drive.

Naturally, I stopped to say hello, and he said, "Come with me . . . just for a couple of minutes."

"I'm on my way home, Dennis," I said, trying to beg off.

"Please, I need you to come with me to the house."

Dennis was by that time separated from Carol, but he was having a hard time accepting the fact that she wanted a divorce, which was a very understandable situation from Carol's point of view, since Dennis was far from being a very stable person.

The last time I was at his home on Benedict Canyon, he handed me a shotgun and asked, "Have you ever shot one? I just bought this and I'm learning to shoot."

I confessed that I had never fired a shotgun, although I added I had been a pretty fair shot with a rifle. He insisted I try it. I said,

"Where?" He said, "In the back yard." I tried to explain that it was illegal to shoot any kind of firearms in the city and especially in Beverly Hills.

He said, "Heck, I do it all the time. The cops never bother me."

With Dennis, when he wanted you to do something, the easiest thing to do was do it. So, I went with him into the back yard, where he had a target set up on the far side of the pool. I took my one shot, said, "That was quite an experience, Dennis. We should do it again sometime."

About the time he bought the gun, Dennis acquired a couple of pets: otters, which were not at all trained, especially with regard to use of the toilet. They usually stayed on the large service porch, which was generally ankle deep in otter crap. They were frolicking in the pool at the time we went to shoot the gun. As pets go, they were pretty much a bust because they didn't seem to like Dennis much.

I went down to the house with Dennis, we pulled into the driveway, and then we went inside. He still had a key. In the den was a young man unknown to either of us. Dennis wanted to know who he was, and he said he was waiting for Carol because they had a date. Dennis was not happy.

Carol was, at that precise moment, still in the bathtub in the master bedroom suite, which was where Dennis headed full tilt. I thought it best to stay in the den, because I liked Carol and didn't want to get involved. The young man was by that time pretty nervous. He thought that it might be best if he left, but I told him to sit still; Carol would handle it and when Dennis left, they could go out and have a good time. I'm sure he spent the rest of the night looking over his shoulder.

I heard Dennis pounding on the bathroom door, demanding to be allowed in, and I could hear Carol shouting at him to go away, to get lost, and to get the hell out of the house.

Dennis was getting pretty loud himself, and I thought it would be prudent if I went back to calm him down. I arrived in the bedroom just a few seconds after he would have smashed the bathroom door in. By the time I arrived, he was sitting calmly on the commode, telling Carol he still loved her and asking her if he could throw her date out of the house.

She was busy wrapping herself in a bath towel when I got there, and was yelling at him to "get the fuck out of the house before I call the cops."

She turned to me and said, "Jack, get this idiot out of here." When I first met Carol back in Kansas City, she was wearing little more than a towel, so she had no qualms about her state of undress.

"C'mon Dennis," I said, as I was dragging him. "Let's get the hell out of here. She doesn't want you around right now. Give her a chance to cool down and then call her." He went with me quietly except that he insisted on stopping in the den first to warn her date that he had better not try anything with Carol or he'd find him and kill him.

Much later, I heard that Dennis married a girl named Barbara. I had never met her and knew nothing at all about her or their relationship, except that someone told me the marriage didn't last very long; long enough, however, for her to get pregnant.

Early one evening, I was for some reason in a Beverly Hills bar and someone introduced me to the gorgeous female bartender, identifying her as Barbara Wilson. I asked if she happened to be the Barbara who married Dennis Wilson.

She exploded, unleashing a string of invective that would have done Richard Nixon proud. Her outburst was followed by, "If you're a friend of that sonofabitch, get the hell out of my bar."

I explained that I only worked for them and that I hadn't seen him in a long time, so she let me have my drink. She didn't throw me out. I never ran into her again and never heard anything more about her.

One more thing about Dennis pops into my mind. He told me that when Mike and Suzanne were getting a divorce, Mike wanted custody of their children. He argued that she was a drug user, which I knew to be true, at least to the extent that she was a regular at the Steve Gold LSD (etc.) parties. However, he had to have proof or something on her or he was certain she would get the kids.

Dennis told me he talked Suzanne into going to Hawaii with him for a week and they spent most of their time in bed together. Then he testified, or threatened to testify, against her to prove Mike's claim that she was an unfit mother. I have no idea whether or not Dennis told me the truth, but that was the last personal contact I had with him. Mike did end up with the kids, so perhaps there was something to it.

CODA

I have wondered how to put an end to my relationship with The Beach Boys. If you've read this far, you already know it didn't just end when I left American Productions. Nick Grillo and Dick Duryea were gone not too long after I left, and although I had occasional contact with Dick, except for the concerts I've already talked about, the meeting with then Secretary of State, Jerry Brown, and my brief contact with Bruce Johnston after Dennis died, I've had no contact with them. I take that back. I did see Alan Jardine at the Bob Hope golf tournament at Pebble Beach, California, but that's in another book.

I should say that my association with Irving Granz and The Beach Boys sent me off on a totally unexpected journey. I went from being a very straight-arrow business type to a player in the world of entertainment. Later, after The Beach Boys, I even became known with my next employer as the company "straight." I suppose it all depends on the rest of the cast of characters with whom you're cast.

Any way, my time with The Beach Boys widened my own horizons. What I learned to do probably eased the way into the next phase of my life. It certainly made me more comfortable in my own skin. In any event, it led me to more adventures that really continue to this day, as the "manager" for a bunch of musicians all close to or even older that I, musicians who were part of the creation of the "Swing Era" of popular music. So you see, life not only goes on, but if you allow it, it can get even more interesting. I guess I owe a debt of thanks to The Beach Boys for allowing me to ride with them for at least a part of their endless summer.

Index

9 781593 931131